eBay 2016

Grow your Business Social Media, Email Marketing, and Crowdfunding

Copyright © 2015 by Nick Vulich

Table of Contents

Read This First

Most books about eBay talk about what to sell or how to sell. This book is going to take a slightly different approach.

I am going to show you how to determine which items sell best on eBay, but I'm not going to say "hey—sell this, don't sell that." Instead I'm going to give you the tools you need to determine which items sell best on eBay, so you can make smart choices about what you should and shouldn't sell.

I'm also going to buck the trend of short forty to fifty page books. No matter how much I've chopped and cut, this book keeps stretching close to the 200 page mark. So if you're looking for a short read, I apologize. But, if you do take the time to read and implement the strategies presented in this book you will see your eBay sales shoot up.

I've conducted a lot of research for this book. To bring it altogether I talked with dozens of experts in email marketing, social media marketing, and Kickstarter crowdfunding campaigns, and just everyday eBay sellers. They all have a story to tell. Some have had more success than others, but one thing I think they will all agree on is the ecommerce marketplace is changing. eBay isn't the same platform it was fifteen years ago when I got started selling there. It's not the same robust platform it was two years ago.

Now that sales have cooled off I wish I would have begun capturing customer emails ten years ago when I was making six hundred to eight hundred sales per month. That would change the whole dynamic. But, guess what? I didn't do that. I didn't jump into social media marketing when it blasted onto the scene. Today I could kick myself for that.

Maybe some of you reading this book feel the same way.

But the way I see it as an eBay seller today, I only have two choices.

1. I can piss and moan like a lot of ex-eBay sellers you see online, and complain that the best days are gone and John Donahoe and company ruined my business.

2. I can come out fighting, make the right moves now, and put control of my business back into my own hands. That way, no matter what eBay does or doesn't do, they can't negatively impact my business, because those customers who deal with me are my customers. They choose to shop with me—on or off of eBay, and I'm going to connect with them in as many different ways as possible to make sure they remain my customers.

This book is all about how you can connect with your customers, and ensure they become repeat buyers, and refer their friends to you.

Whether you want to grow and build your eBay business into an online powerhouse, or just make a few extra sales every month, **eBay 2016** can help you move in the right direction.

. . . .

Last year eBay divulged they are dividing the company into two separate units—eBay and PayPal. To the delight of many eBay sellers, they also announced John Donahoe is being replaced as CEO of eBay. (For a lot of sellers the announcement came as an early Christmas present; for other sellers it came several years too late to do them any good.)

The focus for most sellers right now is to stay in compliance with eBay's new seller standards. The Fall Seller Update was a real bear, and it knocked sellers for a loop. The biggest change is the way eBay evaluates sellers. Instead of evaluating seller performance based strictly on buyer feedback, they now evaluate sellers based upon their defect rate.

For now, I'm going to give a short list of actions that can trigger a seller defect.

- If a buyer leaves a 1, 2, or 3 rating for "item as described."

- A detailed seller rating of one for "shipping time."

- Receiving a negative or neutral feedback.

- Any request to return an item that implies the item is "not as described."

- A seller opening an eBay or PayPal Money Back Guarantee for an item.

- A seller cancelled transaction for any reason.

If a seller has too many defects in either a three month or twelve month period (depending upon how they're evaluated) eBay can restrict or revoke your selling privileges.

As I'm writing this several eBay blogs are already recounting stories of long time Power Sellers and Top Rated Sellers who have had their selling privileges revoked or restricted. Many of these sellers mention that until the new policies went into effect they were compliant with eBay's selling standards and enjoyed Five Star Feedback. The few letters I've seen from eBay, mention the seller is no longer allowed to sell on eBay, but they should still feel free to make purchases.

It seems sort of Dr. Jekyll and Mr. Hyde like—"We don't want you to sell on eBay any more, but, oh—by the way feel free to spend your money and buy more stuff."

Why listen to me?

H ey there, Nick Vulich here.

If you're like me, I'm sure you're probably a little skeptical about taking advice from someone without knowing a little bit about them first.

I've been selling on eBay since 1999. Most of my online customers know me as history-bytes. I've also operated as its old news, back door video, and sports card one.

I've sold 30,004 items for a total of $411,755.44 over the past fifteen years, and that's just on my history-bytes id. I've cut way back on eBay selling over the past year so I can focus on my writing, but I still keep my hat in the game. That way I can keep current with the challenges my readers face every day when they go to sell on eBay.

I've been an eBay Power Seller or Top Rated Seller for most of the past fifteen years, which means I've met eBay's sales and customer satisfaction goals.

This is the eighth book I've written about selling on eBay. The first two, *Freaking Idiots Guide to Selling on eBay*, and *eBay Unleashed*, are aimed more towards how to get started selling on eBay. *eBay Subject Matter Expert* suggests a different approach to selling on eBay – building a platform where customers recognize you as an expert in your niche, and buy from you because of your knowledge in that field. *Sell It Online* gives a brief overview of selling on eBay, Amazon, Etsy, and Fiver. *How to*

Make Money Selling Old Books & Magazines on eBay talks specifically about what I know best, how to sell books and magazines on eBay. *eBay Bookkeeping Made Easy* helps sellers understand how to keep track of the money they are making, and how to take advantage of the tax code to make even more money. *eBay Shipping Simplified* helps sellers determine the best way to ship their items, and how to use eBay's shipping tools to make the task easier. It also has a primer on international shipping, and using third party shipping providers such as Stamps.com and Endicia.

eBay 2015 (also known as *eBay Business Advanced*) is my longest book to date, and encapsulates everything sellers need to know to start and grow their eBay business.

If you didn't read the first section of this book, I'm going to repeat— I'm not going to tell you what sells best on eBay. That info changes from day to day. You've probably heard the old saying, "You can lead a horse to water, but you can't make it drink." In this case, I'm going to teach you how to pick items that are consistently good sellers. This way you're not dependent upon a list of items someone else said sold well for them.

The majority of this book is focused on marketing and promotion because that's where eBay is falling down right now.

Last year eBay stopped all of their Google Pay-Per-Click (PPC) advertising because they didn't think it was effective. Translation—the ads were expensive, and eBay didn't want to * invest * the money necessary to help your items get found in search.

Here's the truth. eBay is one of many ecommerce platforms you can choose from to list your merchandise on. It's up to you to find your own customers.

Let me repeat that. If you want to be successful selling on eBay, Amazon, Etsy, or wherever today—it's up to you to find your own customers.

That's kind of scary when you start to think about it. But, it's also empowering, because it puts you in the driver's seat, and lets you take control of your own destiny.

I'm going to talk about several specific forms of marketing that can help you grow your eBay business.

1. Email marketing
2. Social Media Marketing
3. Blogging
4. Crowd Funding with Kickstarter

You don't need to try them all at once to be successful, but you do need to understand them. All four items are components of the new business paradigm.

They're about being social and connecting with your customers on a whole new level, rather than just trying to sell them something.

You need to shift out of that "one and done" mentality, and move on to really connecting with your customers and becoming a normal part of their day-to-day routine.

Like I said—it's scary, but it's all in how you approach it. Done properly the marketing techniques you learn from this book will take your online business to a whole new level—one where your customers see you as a trusted friend and expert—or, if you look at it on a more basic level you need to position yourself as their "go to guy."

My goal is to help you become as successful as you wish to be.

Let's get started...

Example 1 – Using Advanced Search

L et's look at an example.

The first thing you need to do is pick a category to sell in. To make it easier, we're going to eliminate electronics, cell phones, and name brand clothing. They're all big sellers on eBay, but unless you have an inside track to sourcing new product, it's next to impossible to make money in these hyper-competitive categories.

The iPhone 6 was one of the hottest products on the market for the last Christmas season. Most retailers couldn't get their hands on any of the 64K or 128K models. The 16K phones were readily available, and they sold like hot cakes.

Most of us don't have the cash it takes to make a go at selling the iPhone 6, but a quick look through eBay shows a fast paced market in iPhone 6 accessories.

For this example we're going to look at iPhone 6 cases and determine where the market is so we can optimize our sales by only offering the fastest moving products. To do this we're going to use the advanced search tool to narrow down our choices.

A quick search on eBay shows…

- 1,078,902 completed listings
- 259,634 sold items

- This tells us that roughly 24 % of the items we list are going to sell, or conversely 76 % of the iPhone 6 cases we list aren't going to sell.

Now let's break it down by price range.

- $ 0 to $ 10
- 205,715 sales
- 148,632 sold at auction
- 64,175 sold with Buy It Now

- $ 10 to $ 25
- 37,067 sales
- 11,190 sold at auction
- 25,750 sold with Buy It Now

- $ 25 to $50
- 13,759 sales
- 3794 sold at auction
- 10,254 sold with Buy It Now

- $50 to $100
- 1840 sales
- 685 sold at auction

- 1191 sold with Buy It Now

- $1000 to $2500
- 142 sales
- 98 sold at auction
- 46 sold with Buy It Now

A couple of interesting things pop out when you examine this list. More items sold at auction on the high and low end of the price spectrum. In the mid-range, more items sold using Buy It Now. This tells you the best listing format to use for your iPhone 6 cases.

The raw sales data can also help us select the right price range to sell in.

In this case, I chose the $25 to $50 price range. It had strong sales – 13,759 cases sold out of 28,534 listed. That's a 46 % sell through rate; almost double that of the category as a whole.

Now we can take it a step further and select the top selling brands.

- Otterbox 3,886
- Michael Kors 1,031
- Gorilla Glass 268

Don't forget, you can do this in any category. When you do an advanced search by price point, brand, size, or some other parameter, you are more likely to choose items that are really going to sell.

If you do this every time, you're going to sell more items at a higher price point.

. . . .

Now that we've picked an item to sell, it's time to investigate the best way to sell it.

The Otterbox is the number one seller in the $25 to $50 price range. It comes in three varieties: the Defender, the Commuter, and the Symmetry. Using the advanced search tool we can pull up the listings that sold at higher prices to see what those sellers did different. Sometimes it's as simple as using more effective keywords in the title, more and better pictures, a stronger description, or maybe a combination of all three.

Let's look at the title first. For this example, we're going to use the Otterbox Defender.

Here are some of the keywords included in the top selling listings:

- New
- Case and Belt Clip Holster
- iPhone 6
- Otterbox Defender Case
- Pink, Gray, Glacier, Black
- Authentic / 100 % Genuine
- Free 2-3 Day Shipping
- Case Cover Skin

Okay. We've got 80 characters to work with, so a great title would look something like this.

- Otterbox Defender Case for iPhone 6 New 100 % Authentic Black

- New Otterbox Defender Case for iPhone 6 with Belt Clip & Holster

- New Otterbox Defender Case for iPhone 6 **FREE 2 Day Shipping **

That's how you write a great selling title.

Examine the top selling listings. Pick and choose the hot keywords, and craft a title that jumps your listing over the competition.

Example 2 – Using Advanced Search

This time were going to take an everyday item many sellers list on eBay.

Party supplies.

A number of sellers I know sell party packs—party hats, favors, napkins, treat bags, paper plates, and piñatas. They purchase their inventory from online suppliers, from closeouts bins at local party stores, and even from large discount stores like Walmart and Target.

The trick to making money is to know which items eBayers are buying now.

The first step is to do a general advanced search. In this case the broad term we're going to search on is party supplies. That brings up 418,033 listings. When we search on sold listings we see that 102,448 listings closed successfully, or sold. That gives us a sell through rate of just over 24 percent. Right off the bat that tells us this is going to be a tough category to make money in because 76 percent of all listings don't sell.

Now we can narrow it down further by seeing which items sell the best.

- Sponge Bob
- 337 sales
- 96 sold with auction
- 241 sold with buy it now

- Frozen
- 7629 sales
- 3596 sold with auction
- 4034 sold with buy it now

- Ninja Turtles
- 642 sales
- 120 with auction
- 522 sold with buy it now

- Cars
- 966 sales
- 317 sold with auction
- 649 sold with buy it now

- Elmo
- 291 sales
- 52 sold with auction
- 239 sold with buy it now

- Cat in the Hat
- 117 sales
- 25 sold with auction
- 92 sold with buy it now

- Spiderman
- 691 sales
- 154 sold with auction
- 537 sold with buy it now

- How to Train Your Dragon
- 117 sales
- 25 sold with auction
- 92 sold with buy it now

The first thing that pops out at me when I examine these numbers is party supplies isn't a hot selling or big money category. Many of the items listed there sell in the five to ten dollar range, with a few items stretching to twenty-five dollars or more each. Frozen, Cars, and Ninja Turtles are the hot franchises where the money is right now, so that's where you should concentrate your listings. Just remember the category appears to be driven by bestselling movies, so keep an eye on what new cartoons are around the corner, and be ready to jump on them while they're hot.

Another interesting tid-bit is old standbys like Bugs Bunny and the other Looney Tunes characters don't sell well.

The same goes for the hot FOX series like the Simpsons and American Dad. Sellers should take this as a warning. Just because something is popular, doesn't mean it's an item that is going to sell well in the party supplies category. Another big name item that surprised me was Shrek. Shrek was a huge selling franchise, but right now the party supply market for it is non-existent.

I wouldn't make a move in this category without researching what's selling, and I definitely wouldn't make any large buys. The market appears quite fickle, and when a new bestseller pops onto the scene even Frozen could be knocked out of its top place rather quickly.

As for selling methods, buy-it-now listings outsold auction listings for every item I examined. Stick to buy-it-now listings to maximize your sales and profits. Use auctions to clear out slow selling inventory.

I hope this helps you understand how to research what sells best.

You don't need to perform any complicated computations, but you should take more than a few minutes to explore any category you're planning on jumping into. Make sure it's a strong overall category, and that you're focusing on the bestselling segments of that market.

Even if you give in and pick a weaker category to sell in such as party supplies, you should be able to scratch out a decent profit if you focus on selling the right items.

This means you need to do your research before you purchase anything to resell.

Use Advanced Search to Create Better Selling Listings

Pictures are a key ingredient when you are crafting a top selling listing.

If you want to make more sales you need to check out what the top sellers in your category are doing. How many pictures do they use in each listing? What angles do they show the item from? Do they have drawings, showing how the case is constructed, and how it's put together? What about colors? Do they show just one? Or do they have a picture showing all of the different colors available?

Write a Benefits Driven Description

Next, we need to look at the description.

Balance the length of your description against the way people read on the internet.

People have short attention spans, so it's best to keep your description short. Two to three paragraphs is good. Any more, and you'll start to lose a potential buyer's interest.

Use headlines, short two or three sentence paragraphs, and bullet points to list any item specifics. Include plenty of white space.

Focus more on benefits than on features. Too many sellers write a long list of features thinking that's why people buy stuff, but they're mistaken about that. People want to know what's in it for them. They buy stuff because of what it will do for them.

People buy things that –

1. Save them time
2. Make them more money
3. Help them lose weight
4. Find love
5. Look better

Take a look at this list every time you write a new product description, and use it to help you create more benefit driven descriptions.

Here are a couple examples to help you word your benefit statements.

- You're new Kindle practically reads the book for you. With the new Whisper Synch technology you can read the book when it's convenient, and have it read the book to you while you're driving, taking a long soak in the tub, or at the gym working out.

- This TV comes with a smart remote that lets you operate it with your voice alone. No more fumbling for on / off or channel control buttons in the dark.

Do the same thing with every item you're selling. Pick out one or two features customers really want, and tell them how those features can benefit them.

Do it with every listing and you'll sell more items—guaranteed!

How do top sellers word their listings? Are they HTML formatted, or do they use fancy listing templates? What kind of illustrations do they include on the listing page? Do they use graphics to illustrate free shipping, a 100 % money back guarantee, or a clip from their feedback?

You don't want to outright copy any one seller. Instead you want to pick and choose the best elements from each listing. If you see a free shipping graphic you like, check out a clip art site, and choose a high impact graphic that one ups the site you're trying to emulate.

Some of the sellers have custom graphics that show how the case or packaging snaps or screws together. Think about how you can do something similar. It's easy to find a designer on *Fiverr* or *elance* that will put together a great image for under fifty bucks.

Here's the way I'd approach it.

Pick out two or three drawings your competitors are using. Send them to your designer, along with one or two ideas to personalize it for your business. That keeps you free from copyright violation, and personalizes the illustration for your business.

If your competitors are all using a custom listing template, there are a couple ways you can approach the situation. You can shell out five hundred or one thousand bucks for your own fancy template, or you can try a less expensive workaround.

Most recently I opted to go with two listing headers for each of my listings. One is posted at the top of the listing, and the other at the bottom. All told, they cost me about fifteen bucks on Fiverr, and they give my listings a unique look.

This one goes at the top of my listings. It's a plug for me, my books, and it lets customers know they can save $15.00 if they spend $50.00.

The bottom banner tells prospective buyers more about my business, and emphasizes that we offer free shipping, and a 14 Day Money Back Guarantee. I place this banner at the bottom of every listing because it helps close the deal by letting potential buyers know there is little or no risk involved in doing business with me.

- 15 years of experience selling on eBay
- 30,000 happy buyers
- 100 % positive feedback

If you don't take anything else away from reading this section, remember that you need to research every item before you post it on eBay.

Yeah. Most anything will sell if you give it enough time, but if you pick the right items to list and sell, you're going to save yourself a lot of frustration, and you're going to make more sales that close in a higher price range. You're also going to save money on listing fees by picking items to sell that have a stronger sell through rate.

Price Your Items to Sell

Pricing is one of the trickiest parts of selling on eBay or any online site.

If you price your item too high no one will buy it. If you price your item too low you could be leaving profit on the table. The problem is there's no one hundred percent perfect method for pricing your item right out of the box. Pricing is more of a process, especially if you're selling multiples of an item.

The easiest way to price your item is to search eBay to see what similar items have recently sold for. To do this you need to use the advanced search function.

To access the Advanced Search function, go to the top of the eBay page. To the right of the search box you will see the word **Advanced** just after the big blue Search box. Go ahead and click on the word **Advanced**.

Type in the name or description of the item you want to search for. Scroll down a little further to where it says **search including** and check the box by **Completed Listings**. Then click enter. This will return a list of all the ended listing for that item within the past thirty days. Items listed in green are items that have sold.

After you've done this you'll see a list of completed items. And, the great thing is it shows you how much items similar to yours have recently sold for on eBay.

There's no need to guess. A quick look through the completed listings will give you the exact price range your item has recently sold in.

What I do is look through the titles to find items most similar to mine. Each time I click into an item I note the price it sold for. If it sold at auction, I mark down the starting price. After you do this four or five times you know the price range you can expect your item to sell in.

At this point we're almost ready to start pricing our item.

Before you stop doing your research, click into two or three of the items that sold at a higher price point. Did the seller start the item at a lower price or use buy-it-now.

Now you have the information you need to determine a pricing strategy.

Some sellers swear by starting everything at 99 cents or $9.99 and letting the market determine the price. The problem with this strategy is it only works for certain categories of items. If you sell something that always closes in a tight price range like electronics, cell phones, iPhones, iPads, and the like, starting your item at 99 cents is going to bring in the maximum number of bidders, and will normally bring you the highest possible price for each item.

If you sell one of a kind items—collectibles, and other low demand items, starting your item at 99 cents is a recipe for disaster. What's going to happen in nine out of ten cases is, if your item sells at all, it's going to sell for 99 cents, or $1.04.

A better strategy is to price your item at the lowest price you're willing to accept, and then add a buy-it-now at what you would like to get. If you're selling your item in a fixed price format, set the price somewhat higher than you hope to get, and add best-offer.

What if you're selling something unique, that isn't currently available on eBay? How do you price your item then?

If it's something you have a lot of, or a lot of similar items the best thing you can do is experiment with different prices, and determine which one sells the most items.

Let me give you an example. I sell old magazine articles, removed from bound magazines. So basically, all I'm selling is a few sheets of old paper. I have a few competitors on eBay, but not many.

When I first started selling magazine articles back in 2000, I priced all of my items at $12.99, and they sold really well.

After about six months I increased my price to $15.99, and then $19.99, and then $25.99, and sales kept increasing each time. When I stretched it again to $27.99, sales started slowing down. As a result, I knew my optimal price range was somewhere between $19.99 and $25.99.

I found my sweet spot in auction pricing the same way. I started my items at $9.99 and many of them sold. Then I added Buy-it-Now at 15.99, $19.99, and $25.99. Once again $25.99 provided the most conversions, so that's the formula I went with – a $9.99 starting price, with a $25.99 Buy-it-Now.

It was a great price strategy and it worked for years.

The next thing you know, eBay decided they wanted to be more like Amazon, and to become more of a marketplace so they could reel in the big box retailers like Best Buy and Toy-R-Us.

One of the things they did was to change the emphasis to fixed price listings rather than auctions. That sent me back to the drawing board, and once again, I reinvented my eBay business, this time focusing it around fixed price listings, with a just a smattering of auction listings.

Email Marketing for Your eBay Business

Here's something many sellers are unaware of: your customers belong to eBay, not you. That's why eBay is so protective about offsite sales and contact. If sellers get their hands on an eBay customer and encourage them to purchase directly from them that's one less sale made on the eBay platform.

So what's the easiest way to capture customers to build an email list for your eBay business? Include a bounce back offer in every package you ship. Make the offer irresistible and inexpensive and you'll increase the number of takers. If you've got a website or blog, display the URLs prominently in your flyers. At the very least, include your email address and social media contact info.

Better yet, include a QR code on every flyer you send out. (If you're not familiar with them, a QR code looks similar to a bar code. Cell phone users can download an app that will read the QR code when they snap a picture of it. As soon as they take a picture of the QR code it will take them to your website or special offer. Don't know how to create one, not a problem. Designers on Fiverr will create a QR code for you for five or ten dollars.)

Give your customers a wide variety of methods to connect with you.

Here's another little secret.

The best way to connect with your customers is through email. Despite what marketers say about email being dead, it's the most effective and inexpensive way to connect with your audience. The trick is to steer away from selling. Instead, share valuable tips and information your customers will need, enjoy, use, and look forward to receiving.

It sounds counterintuitive, but it's true.

Remember the old saying? "You've got to give a little to get a little." The same thing is true in sales. You can ask, beg, and plead with people all day long hoping they will buy from you. Some people will listen to your message, and buy from you. Some won't.

But, if potential customers read about how your product or service helped other people just like them solve their problems, they are more likely to give your offer a shot.

The take away here is to share information.

Share stories from customers who've had success, and enjoyed using your product and service. Write short emails that focus on your niche. It can be a tie in to an upcoming holiday, a new release in your field, a hard to find item everyone in your niche wants. Don't be afraid to share competitor links, especially for one-of-a-kind items. It will make people think you're just not out to get their money, but are truly concerned and interested in them.

The primary rule of email marketing is: to give more than you get.

Share eight to ten tips and stories for every one sales pitch you send out. This makes it more likely readers will continue to open your emails. It also makes them more likely to act on your offers if you're not pitching something in every email you send.

Getting started with email

I have to admit I was a little slow getting started with email marketing, and I could kick myself for it now.

Every piece of advice I've read about selling online says you need an email list. Today, I'm over fifteen years into the game, have made over thirty thousand sales, and have likely thrown away twice that many opportunities to make additional sales.

Think of all the customers I let slip through my fingers.

To be honest, I tried to set up an email list several times. Each time I decided it was just too hard. I didn't understand how to do it, so I kept putting it off. I could always justify it. Sales were good. People were buying my stuff, sometimes by the boatload. So why would I ever need an email list?

Well, over the last two years I discovered one reason I need a list - what goes up, also goes down. My sales have been disheartening, not terrible - but definitely trending downward.

I've run a number of Mark Down Deals, and done some other promos, but they haven't been as effective as usual. I suspect part of this is the time of year. October is horrible for retail sales. They normally pick up the first or second week of November.

The thing is, if I had heeded the advice to build a list, I could have done some targeted marketing to level out my sales.

That's the problem.

Here's the solution.

I set up a list management account with Mail Chimp, and added links to all of my stuff, and to both of my blogs. My goal for the next year is to move from zero to a minimum of twenty-five hundred subscribers for my mail list.

To do that, I'm going to concentrate on doing more promos, designing more effective flyers, and bounce back offers. Most times, my flyers feature items at regular price, or discounted a few bucks. I'm going to shoot for an irresistible offer—something in the five to ten dollar price range.

I'm also going to push the free content on my blogs. This way people don't have to spend a penny to engage with me. They can go to my blog, enjoy my content, check out a few of the items I'm selling, and, hopefully—fill out my mail list sign up form if they enjoy what they see.

Creating an email list with Mail Chimp

H ere's a quick tutorial on how to create a mail list sign up form with Mail Chimp.

The examples are from an article on my indie author's toolbox blog, so please bear with me. The information you see is for my books, but it can be easily adapted to creating an email sign up list for your eBay business.

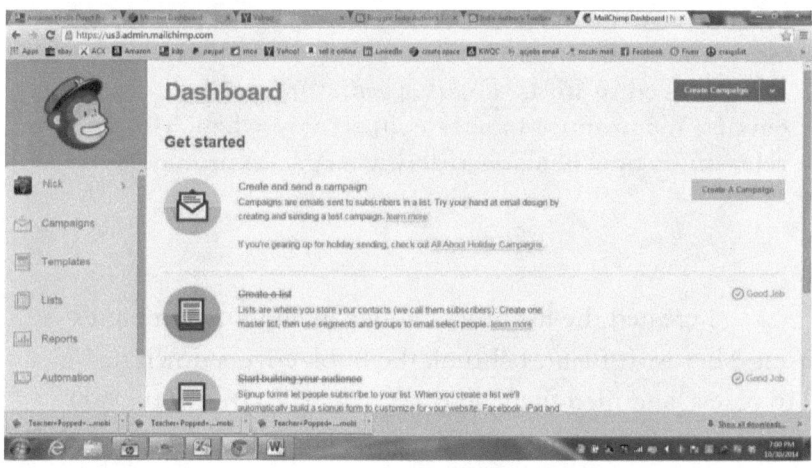

To create your mail list from the Mail Chimp dashboard, select Create-a-list and follow the prompts.

After you have your list set up it's time to create your sign up form. Mail Chimp makes it easy to design a fancy form to entice readers to sign up, or you can go with something Plain Jane. The choice is entirely up to you.

If you enjoy Nick's books, be sure to sign up for our mailing list. You'll be among the first to know when Nick releases a new book.

PS: No need to worry about spam, or receiving a slug of emails. We promise to only contact you when Nick is releasing a new book, or running a special promo.

I created the list header above in about five minutes using Microsoft Paint. I shrunk the book covers down to 175 x 116 pixels, and tiled them across a rectangle sized 700 x 600 pixels. I used the line tool to draw the lines above and below the books and typed my text into the space below the covers. Alternatively, you could pay someone on Fiverr and let them design something really fancy.

Here's a screen shot of the actual signup form. It's easy to customize, too. You can easily add or delete fields for the information you want to collect. Remember, you want to make it as easy as possible for readers to sign up. The more information you ask for, the more people are going to decide it's not worth it. My advice is to ask for the email address and first name. It's the path of least resistance.

If you look where it says Grouping 11725, you can see the different categories. This lets buyers choose what they want to be notified about. Readers interested in only my ecommerce or history books can choose just those categories. When I send out offers about my self-publishing books or political humor works they won't be bothered.

Sign up for Nick's mailing list to be notified of any upcoming specials or new releases.

Email Address

First Name

Grouping 11725

☐ ecommerce books

☐ self-publishing books

☐ history books

☐ political humor

☐ fiction

Preferred format

You could create several different lists or signup forms, but this makes it easier to manage your lists.

There are also several options available to embed forms on your blog or website, integrate with a Word Press blog, or create a form to use on Facebook.

To include a link in your book, add the signup form URL to the front or back matter of your book. Here's how I do it.

Want to know about Nick's new book releases? Join our mailing list.

Interested in being notified when Nick releases his next book? Click here to join our mailing list. We promise not to send any spam, or unwanted emails. The only thing you will receive is news about Nick's new book releases, and occasional specials we are offering.

If you don't do any more than this, you should be able to build a good sized mail list over time just from buyer signups.

Another option is to include the signup form on your blog. Select the Embedded Forms option from the Mail Chimp menu. Choose the fields you want to include on your sign-up form, and copy the embed code. Paste the code where you want to embed the signup form on your blog. That's all there is to it. If you have a Word Press blog use the Integrated Forms option to include a signup form on your blog.

Here's a link to my *indie author's toolbox* *www.indieauthorstoolbox.com* blog so you can check out my sign up form. It's visible on every page viewer's checkout, so there are multiple points where they can choose to sign up for my email list.

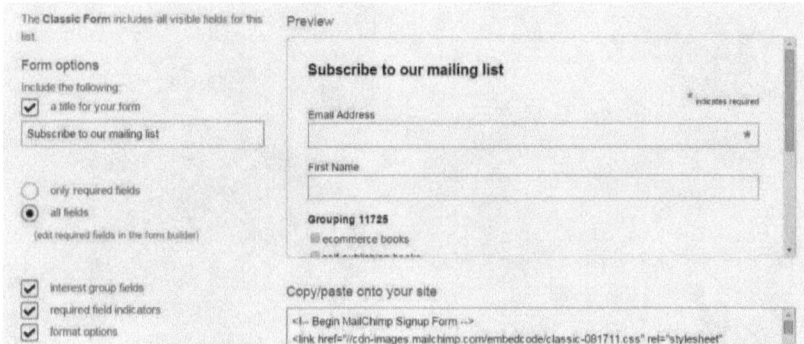

There are also options to add signup forms for you Facebook page or for tablets.

Interview with Rob Cubbon

Rob Cubbon was born in Kent, England. He has been a graphic designer and creative director for print and web since 1995. He started his own company, the imaginatively titled Rob Cubbon Ltd, in 2006 to provide design and marketing services to promote products, businesses and services. More recently he has created e-books and video courses on the subjects of running a web design business, online promotion, web design and passive income. You can visit his website at http://robcubbon.com/.

Email marketing is a little trickier for eBay sellers than many other online sellers. eBay is very protective of their customers and prohibits most outside communications with sellers because they don't want to encourage offsite sales. I encourage sellers to include flyers with links to their websites, social media sites, and blogs. Can you think of

any other ways for sellers to direct customers to their email signup page?

I agree flyers with a link to your website are a great idea. But, why should the customer rush to their device and visit the site? You have to offer something of value to the customer as an incentive to visit a particular page. So offer something for free – a free e-book, free video course, free updates and information – relevant to the product. You will get many more sign ups that way.

. . . .

Mail Chimp offers some good tools that let sellers create nice looking sign up pages? What elements do you feel are essential to a good sign up page? Is the key to more signups an amazing graphic, video, convincing text…or is it a combination of all three?

Less is more. Try to take everything out of a sign-up page that isn't necessary. Definitely remove all links off the page (so out goes the header (with links to the home page, the blog page, the contact page, etc.); out goes the sidebar; out goes the footer) so you're left with the offer with an image and the sign up form. That's it. Nothing more. So visitors either leave their email or they leave.

. . . .

I know Facebook has an option on business pages where sellers can link to their email signup form. Do you have any advice for sellers on how to implement and use that feature?

No, I don't do things like this. I don't think people visit Facebook Pages much. It's more about getting them to Like the Page and then to engage them going forward.

. . . .

What types of info should sellers send to their email list? I've had sellers tell me 90 % of what they send out is product information, discounts, and notices about upcoming sales. Is that too much selling, and not enough sharing? Or, is there any hard and fast rule about the types of email sellers should send out?

There's probably no hard and fast rule, and every niche and every business is different. Personally, I like to give value emails (ie. emails with no selling only helpful information) two or three times before a sales email. However, sales emails often have "reminder emails" following up so you will inevitably have two – or even three – sales emails in a row. But I like to follow that with a lot of value.

I know a lot of other list owners who have huge volume that might be more "aggressive" than me in terms of selling.

. . . .

I receive a lot of email communications from other sellers, authors, etc. Most of it is all over the board. Some of it is plain text, with a link to an article or video. Some of it is full blown html, beautifully coded with graphics and video. And, sometimes it is just a short message, with a link to the sender's blog or website. What works best? Or does it depend on what you're trying to communicate?

I've always avoided the completely designed email – it's hard to do, it costs more, it's more likely to be held in a spam folder and there's no evidence if it converts. Plain text emails look like the normal emails we get and I like that. At the same time I like to include a logo and an image of my signature but that's just me!

. . . .

How much is too much? Can you send too much stuff to your email list? I've signed up for some lists and have gotten as many as ten to twelve messages the first month. That makes me want to unsubscribe, so what I guess I'm asking is—where do you draw the line between not enough, and too much?

"Ten to twelve messages the first month" – that's nothing? I was talking to a marketer in the crypto-currency niche who sends emails every day. And he's a hugely successful email marketer. Again, it's a different niche and he has volume.

The "not enough" question is easier to answer. I wouldn't leave it longer than two weeks because I know from experience that people will forget who you are and report you for spam and, remember, companies like Mail Chimp will not think twice about banning your account if you have only two or three spam complaints.

. . . .

How about auto-responders? When most people talk about email marketing they talk about putting your marketing on autopilot. You have a pre-programmed set of emails setup to go out to customers to welcome them into the fold, and then get them on a regular email cycle. Could you talk a little bit about auto responders, and why or why not sellers would want to use them?

I would definitely suggest everyone uses them because they build up a relationship with a list and get you sales on auto-pilot. They save time.

However, they are not the be all and end all. It doesn't matter how many emails you have in your auto-responder sequence, one day they will be finished for the subscriber and that's why you have to keep on sending out the broadcast emails.

Typically my sequence follows the same sequence of jab, jab, jab, right hook – so three or four value emails followed by a sales offer. And you can repeat that over and over.

. . . .

I understand you're not an eBay seller so this may not be an easy question to answer, but I think it's important to what we're talking about here. eBay has what's called a Mark Down Manager that allows sellers to discount their product line for a certain period of time. What would be the best way for sellers to let potential buyers know about sales? Do they build excitement beforehand? Do they send out a string of emails—announcing the sale, midway through, and again letting them know it's almost over? Or is one email enough?

I'm not an eBay seller but I can certainly attest to the importance of building up excitement before a sale. Just presenting an email list – or any audience – with an offer is a rookie mistake.

People sometimes need to be presented with an offer 7 or 8 times before they purchase. So you have to get creative with reasons to mention the offer.

Ask questions about the new product; do a survey about what the customer wants; post images in social media of the product being created; ask customers to help you with the name, logo, packaging; run competitions; create multiple offers and bundles at different times… the list goes on.

But, whatever you do, don't just introduce an offer with no lead up.

. . . .

What's better, sending out an informational email about a new product, a sale notice, or a combination of both?

Going along with what I was saying earlier, it would be information first; sale notice second.

. . . .

Last question, what else do you feel sellers must know to be successful with email marketing?

There are so many facets to email marketing. It's difficult to know where to start.

Here are a few tips that have worked for me:

- *Create multiple landing pages with different free offers to gather email addresses not just one*
- *Create redirects so that the URLs of the landing pages are easy to remember, eg. http://robcubbon.com/free ; http://robcubbon.com/freecourse ; etc.*
- *Make the email looking like an ordinary email as much as possible. So, make sure it's from a real person "Rob Cubbon", for example, not "Acme Corp Ltd."*
- *Fix the width of the email so it's around 400 pixels wide but otherwise don't start messing around with designed HTML emails or images much*

- *Create short paragraphs in the email – hardly ever more than 2 sentences – and keep it to the point.*
- *Your email list is one of your most important business assets. Treat it with great care.*
- *The email list is for building trust, awareness and a business relationship first; selling second.*

Social Media Marketing for eBay Sellers

D o you really need to blow up social media to sell on eBay and Amazon?

It's sort of like asking, are you a glass is half full, or a glass is half empty type of person. If you're a glass is half full type, you're going to scream "Damn right! You have to be on social media, because—that's where the people are." If you're a glass is half empty type you're going to whine and moan "what's the point? I'm selling my stuff on eBay, not on Facebook and Twitter."

You probably see where I'm going with this.

Online sellers are divided on the need for social media, its uses, and its outcomes. Some sellers will tell you they couldn't have gotten where they are without it, others will say "Why bother!" or "Hey! I tried it, and it didn't make any diff. My sales stayed the same."

I'm going to try not to take sides here. My goal is to give you the information you need to implement social media in your eBay business should you choose to do so.

My primary focus is going to be on Facebook, Twitter, and Pinterest because they are the three powerhouses behind social media today. Facebook and Twitter get a bigger mention because they are the social media sites everybody goes to. Pinterest gets a bigger mention because it is the one seller's say actually works best.

Does that mean you need to use all three? Or that you should focus exclusively on Pinterest because it's what works best for most sellers? No. It means you should start out slow. Pick one or two social media platforms and spend ten or fifteen minutes on them two or three days a week.

A PEW University study on social media usage has one more relevant piece of information for savvy online marketers— over half of the people who visit social media sites are active on more than one site. For marketers the implication is clear, if you want to reach your primary customer base, you need to be active on several social media platforms. Using one social media platform isn't going to cut it. Think a minimum of two, maybe even three social media platforms if you want to reach your target audience effectively.

When you are first getting started watch what other sellers in businesses similar to yours are doing on social media sites. Like some of their posts and start building your network. Make a few short posts. Put up a few pictures, or some short videos. Rinse and repeat.

The key to success with social media is to post regularly, comment when someone likes or comments on one of your posts, and keep a conversation going with your followers. Over time you will develop a following of your own.

And, one other tip, don't try to move too quickly, or fast track your way to success. There are a lot of places on and off of eBay where you can purchase 500 or 1,000 likes. Don't be tempted. Phantom fans who don't comment on your posts, or like them, aren't going to do your business any good over the long haul.

Remember, it's not a contest to see who can get the most followers. It's all about getting the most followers who will engage with you on a regular basis, and who will share your content with their friends and followers.

That's how you build your business using social media. Give more than you get, share content your followers like, enjoy, and can use. If you do this, sales will follow.

Social Media by the Numbers

ccording to a *PEW University study* published in 2014 seventy-one percent of adults who use the internet are on Facebook. Twitter, LinkedIn, Instagram, and Pinterest lag way behind with adult usage rates that fall somewhere between 23 to 28 percent.

Here are a few key takeaways for anyone planning to use social media to grow their online business.

- 31 percent of seniors are on Facebook.
- 53 percent of young adults age 18 to 29 are on Instagram. And, over half of these users visit the site daily.
- Women are three times as likely to use Pinterest as men. 42 percent of women who use the internet are on Pinterest, versus 13 percent of men.

If you need more help in choosing the correct social media platform to reach your key demographics check out the rest of the *PEW University study*. *http://www.pewinternet.org/2015/01/09/social-media-update-2014/*

Facebook users are aging with a larger percentage of seniors over age sixty-five on the site. Women are more likely to frequent Facebook than men.

Twitter usage is higher among young adults ages eighteen to twenty-nine, and falls off sharply among users over age forty-nine. Young adults and Afro-Americans are more likely to engage on Twitter.

Instagram has a high usage rate among young Americans ages eighteen to twenty-nine, and among Afro-Americans.

Pinterest users are primarily women, who tend to be college educated and more affluent.

LinkedIn is used less than other social media sites, but could be helpful if you are marketing to individuals between the ages of fifty to sixty-five. LinkedIn users also tend to be college graduates, with a higher annual household income.

The PEW University study does leave out one important group—teenagers.

If you're marketing primarily to teens you need to check out a 2014 study by Piper Jaffray ... *Taking Stock With Teens – Fall 2014. http://www.piperjaffray.com/3col.aspx?id=3268*

Here is some of the information you will discover.

- You're message better look good on an iPhone, because 67 percent of teenagers either have or plan on getting an iPhone.
- Instagram and Twitter is the social media site most frequented by teens. So if teens are your target audience you need to include more pictures, video, and music in your posts, and fewer words.
- Pinterest is the least used social media site among teens.

- Facebook is used by fifty percent of all teens, but is not as popular as it was in the past.

One more important concept online sellers need to grasp is the people you want to reach spend a large portion of their day online. Many of them rarely if ever leave social media sites, so if you don't engage with them there, you're not going to be able to sell to them—period.

Facebook

Facebook is the big kid on the block in social media marketing. It used to be the "in" site for kids, but now that it has gone main-stream Facebook has become the primary social media platform used by marketers to reach women, age thirty-five to sixty.

If you haven't checked your Facebook News Feed lately one of the first things you'll notice is the changes in the content you see. Many of the top posts shown in your News Feed today are paid spots that Facebook considers relevant to your interests. Your friend's posts are still there, but they're intermixed with paid content Facebook thinks might grab your interest, and make them a few bucks to boot.

Something else you need to understand is the majority of Facebook users access the site only from mobile devices. This means you need to keep your posts short, with quick easy to load pictures and videos. You should also check out every post you make to ensure it looks good on an Android or IOS (Apple) device.

Getting started

Facebook is all about engaging with other users. That means your primary goal is to provide content that makes users want to like, comment on, and share your posts.

How do you do that?

Look at the popular posts in your News Feed, the ones users have liked and shared. The odds are they have at least one thing in common. Nine times out of ten they are visually oriented, which means they contain pictures or videos.

Facebook pictures come in a number of varieties, but they all share one common trait. They're of a person, or a cute furry pet—maybe even a baby. They're of a person making a funny face, or stuck in a strange place, or doing something unusual. Other times it's a picture of someone famous along with one of their quotes.

If you pay attention you will see dozens of similar pictures in your News Feed every week. Some of them are cartoon images with catchy phrases; others are quotes from famous people. Many are product images with tag lines that scream out – "new from" … "on sale now" … "check out our new line of."

These types of images are a great way to catch people's attention, and garner a bunch of quick likes and shares. The thing to remember when creating your own items like these is to keep it legal. Don't just grab pictures you like off of the internet and add a snazzy quote. Make sure the image is copyright free. If you're in doubt the best way to select a "legal" picture is to visit a clip art site and invest a few bucks to pay for one time rights to use the image. Two such sites I use all of the time are *Dollar Photo Club* and *Can Stock Photo*. Most of the images on these sites cost under five bucks, less if you buy multiple credits, and they're easy to manipulate using MS Paint so you can create awesome sharable images.

Videos are hot on social media, and if your video catches on it can go viral quickly and spread across the internet.

Make your videos tasteful and keep them focused on your product line. In my case I sell old books and magazine articles. One video I include in all of my eBay listings is of *Professor Puppet* explaining my business and the types of items I sell. It helps people understand what my business is all about.

Other videos that would complement my product line would be reviews of historical books, how to videos about book and magazine collecting, and special interest videos on historical events. Each of them would promote interest in the types of items I sell.

Earlier in this book in the section on how to determine what sells on eBay I touched on Otterbox cases for the iPhone 6. When I purchased my first Otterbox case I was totally stumped about how to get it apart. Sure it came with a short set of directions in a smattering of different languages, but that wasn't enough to help me install the case. To get my phone inside of my new Otterbox case I had to search YouTube for a quick tutorial. (If you haven't discovered it, the trick to removing that thin outer shell is to slip a credit card underneath and pry it up. Thanks again, YouTube.)

A smart seller would have a similar video on his Facebook page, and in his eBay item listing. It's good customer service, and it's likely to be shared time and again bringing customers back to your eBay listing and Facebook page.

Tip: if you decide to include someone else's video or photo in your listings or on your blog or website—get permission first. Contrary to popular belief, most pictures and videos on the internet are copyrighted so it is illegal to reproduce them without proper permission.

If you sell men's, women's, or children's clothes every new season, or product line you take on gives you the opportunity to add a new video to your Facebook page. If you're unsure how to do this check out *Lauren's Fab Finds* for more ideas.

Create more effective Facebook posts

There is a whole lot of advice available about how to create more effective Facebook posts. Here's a short list that should help you boost audience engagement.

1. Keep your words to a minimum. Social media is constantly evolving and the most effective posts are visually oriented. If you want to maintain user engagement keep any text short—80 to 120 characters should be the max.

2. Don't link to stuff off of Facebook. Facebook users prefer to stay in their own little world.

3. Don't over sell. Facebook users are leery of marketing, and are quick to steer away from sales pitches.

4. Don't post the same content on Facebook that you do on other social media sites. Your followers expect new and exciting content, not yesterday's news, or recycled post from Twitter or your blog. Don't disappoint them.

How to Sell on Facebook

All of this begs the question if people don't like to be sold to on Facebook, how do you get them to buy your stuff?

That's a good question and one smart seller's are working hard to crack. The key is to understand what brings people to social media sites in the first place.

According to an April 2013 study published in *The Atlantic* the number one and three reason people go on social media sites is voyeurism. Facebook is the perfect tool to spy on your neighbors and friends. The catch is: Facebook users are consensual Peeking Tom's. We give each other permission to poke their noses into our back doors.

The number two reason people say they visit social media sites is to relieve boredom. They've got nothing better to do, so they turn to Facebook, Twitter, and similar sites to live vicariously through others.

And, the final reason given for visiting social media sites is to message between friends.

So, there you have it.

1. Voyeurism
2. Boredom
3. Messaging

If you are using social media to reach these people you need to play to these needs.

Every post, picture, and video you place on social media sites needs to take people behind the scenes, and give them a sneak peek of what your business or industry is all about. Make it personal, make it entertaining, show vulnerability, and poke fun at yourself.

At the same time, you need to make sure your posts are engaging. Encourage communication with your social media followers, and schedule time every day to follow up with them. If someone comments on one of your posts, respond to them, even if it's just to say "thanks" or "hi."

If you do these things, your posts will play into the reasons people visit social media sites.

Basics of Facebook Marketing

Create a Facebook Fan Page. Don't use your personal Facebook page. It's unprofessional, and it doesn't give you all of the tools you need to engage with your followers.

It's easy to create a Facebook Fan Page. Go to *https://www.facebook.com/pages/create.php.*

That's going to bring up the following page where you select the category to place your Facebook Fan Page in.

The choices are:

1. Local Business or Place
2. Company, Organization or institution
3. Brand or Product
4. Artist, band, or Public Figure
5. Entertainment
6. Cause, or Community

Select the category that best describes your business. For most online sellers it's going to be local business or place, or brand or product, depending upon how you're trying to promote yourself. If you're an author, artist, or musician choose artist, band, or public figure. It's pretty self-explanatory.

The next step is to set up your Facebook page, and give it a name. Your page name should be a no-brainer. If you have a business name or eBay store name that should be the name of your Facebook page. Make it easy for buyers to find you.

Make sure to fill out the about section, and provide a link to your eBay store so people can easily find you. Add appropriate keywords in the about section. In my case, I sell historical collectibles so I would want to work in several of the following keywords, "vintage historical collectibles—magazine articles, prints, and advertisements." This will make it easier for search engines to locate your page, and for viewers to learn what you're all about.

Another neat feature you will find at the top of your page is the ability to *create a call to action button*. The button gives you a number of different choices including—shop now, contact us, use app, watch video, book now, sign up, or play game. If you're an online seller I'd suggest using shop now and linking to your eBay store, and Sign up with a link to your email list sign up form. If you choose only one call to action make it the sign up form for your email list. It will give you the biggest bang for your buck over the long haul.

Create an amazing Timeline Cover Photo. This is the rectangular image at the top of your Facebook page. It needs to reach out and grab viewer's attention. It could be one large photo or a collage of smaller photos showing yourself, your employees, or the products you sell. It may also be a good idea to add a tagline or your business name to your Timeline Cover Photo.

Keep in mind it's one of the first things people see when they come to your Facebook page so you want to do your best to make it stand out, and grab people's attention. With that said, here's my best advice—don't do it yourself. Hire a designer on Fiverr or elance to put together a professional design for you.

You also need to create a profile photo. Some sellers use their logo; others use a photo of one of their better selling products. My suggestion is to use a selfie. Studies show people are more likely to engage with photos of people, so give them what they want. Flash a big smile. If your audience would enjoy a joke—stick your tongue out at them, or make a funny face. A lot of sellers get all fancied up and wear a suit or dress. That's okay, but my thought is you should present a more casual appearance. Dress like you normally would. This will make it easier for people to connect with you.

Now it's time to start adding your first posts.

This is what scares a lot of people, but it's one of the easiest parts about creating a Facebook page if you give it some thought. Think about yourself for a moment. What type of content do you enjoy engaging with on Facebook? Chances are you said—videos, pictures, and short entertaining posts.

That's the type of content you need to give your fan page visitors.

Create a couple of short two to three minute videos that explain your business, and talk about the products you sell; introduce your employees; interview a few of your customers, and let them say what they like about doing business with you. Post a few pictures of products you sell. Put up a humorous photo of your dog or cat playing with your computer or crawling out of a packing box. Post a picture of a hot new product you're getting ready to list.

The truth is there are all sorts of things you can post about. You just need to place yourself in your buyer's shoes and figure out what they'd like to know about your business or product line.

eBay Store Apps

There are a number of apps that let you place your eBay store on your Facebook fan page. Some are more feature filled or work better than others, so I'm giving you a list of apps you can explore.

Auction Items Facebook App

https://apps.facebook.com/auctionitems/. This one lets you put your eBay store in a tab on your Facebook fan page. They also have apps available for Etsy and Bonanza store owners.

Easy Social Shop App

http://www.easysocialshop.com/ebay-facebook-shop/. This is another free and easy solution to get started selling on eBay.

StoreYa

http://www.storeya.com/ebay-to-facebook. StoreYa places a tab on your Facebook fan page so you can begin selling immediately. They also have apps that support Shopify, Amazon, Magneto, and WordPress among others.

3D Sellers

http://apps.ebay.com/selling?ViewEAppDetails&stab=3&appType=1 &appId=SocialStore.3dsellers.com. Social Store from 3D Sellers is available in the eBay apps center and lets you add your eBay store to your Facebook fan page.

Boost your Facebook Post

Sometimes your Facebook posts needs a little more oomph to reach more viewers.

I know what you're thinking. "Hey! I'm on Facebook because it's free. What do you mean I have to spend money to get my posts seen?"

I know, it's crazy but it's true. Facebook has created a new way to make money, and part of it involves hiding your posts, or as they would have it—strategically placing them towards the top of a user's News Feed if you kick in a minor contribution to Zuckerberg and Company.

Here's what Facebook says about boosting your post.

Boosted posts appear higher in your News Feed, so there's a better chance you will see them.

You can boost any type of post—video, picture, or text. To boost a post, click on Boost post in the lower left hand corner of the post. After you do that, select the audience demographics you want to see your post, your budget, and the length of time to boost the post.

Pretty simple so far, right?

In most cases, five to fifteen dollars should get you a big enough boost to reach your audience. If it's something really special, like a new product launch, maybe budget forty or fifty dollars. As for the audience, try to narrow the focus to your prime demographic. If it's showing your message is targeted to millions of readers try to narrow it down some. Shoot for something in the range of fifty to one hundred thousand for your target audience. For your time frame you have a choice of one to seven days. If you boost it longer than two or three days you're going to find yourself pushing old news.

Create a Facebook Event to Promote Your Sale

A Facebook event may or may not work for you. The reason I say this is you can only create an event from your personal Facebook page, not from your Facebook fan page.

Don't get discouraged yet.

Promoting an event to your regular Facebook friends can help you introduce a new product line, or try out new ideas you normally wouldn't use with your regular customers.

Think of your event as a marketing test? It's a chance for you to try new things, and for your friends to get a hell of a deal. Promote it to them that way, and it will be a win-win situation for both of you.

If you're unfamiliar with Facebook events, the easiest way to think of it is as an online party invite. I've received them for family reunions, book launch events, and birthday parties.

The great thing about creating a Facebook event is once you set it up, Facebook does all the work for you. It sends out the invites, collects RSVPs, and posts a reminder on their Facebook homepage for everyone who was invited.

The other cool thing is a Facebook event is super easy to create and manage. Here's a link to Facebook's *instructions for creating an event. https://www.facebook.com/help/210413455658361*

Final takeaway

Facebook can be a great way to help grow your business. Like anything else it can become a bottomless pit sucking up all of your time if you're not careful.

To be successful selling on Facebook you need to

1. Have a plan. Know what you want to accomplish. Do you want to make more sales? Encourage email sign ups? Engage more with customers?

2. Budget 15 to 20 minutes a day three or four days a week and stick to that time limit.

3. Be visual. Facebook users respond best to videos and pictures. Give them what they want, and you will be more successful.

4. Don't over-post, or under-post. If you post too often users are going to unfollow you, or turn off your News Feed. If you don't post often enough, people are going to forget who you are. Three to five good posts a week is enough to get your message out there.

5. Spend a few bucks to boost your posts, especially when you're first getting started. It will help you build your audience faster.

6. Find an app to add your eBay store to your Facebook fan page.

7. If you have an email list, link to your sign up form. If you don't have an email list—what are you waiting for?

Twitter

For those of you not familiar with Twitter, it's the social media site with the little blue bird as its symbol. When you feel compelled to communicate with the outside world, you send out a *tweet.*

Tweets are short, sweet, and to the point. There's no room for fluff or excess verbiage. You get 140 characters to tell your story, so you better boil it down to the essentials, and make every character count.

The other cool thing about Twitter is you can share pictures, videos, and links. In fact, if you don't include some visual element in each of your tweets, the odds are no one is going to bother with them. Sorry, but that's another rule of the game you're going to need to get used to.

. . . .

On the face of things, Twitter would appear to be the easiest social media site to master. I mean, you only have 140 characters to work with. All you need to do is punch them out, click send, and your story is let loose upon the world.

If only it were so simple.

The way Twitter works, your message is only seen by your followers and other Twitter users with nothing better to do than search the Twitterverse all day for trending topics.

Your topic is trending, isn't it?

We'll get to that in a bit. For now the very least you need to know is Twitter is one of the social medial powerhouses. According to Twitter they have 288 million users who send out 500 million tweets each and every day. Many of them send out as many as fifty to one hundred tweets per day.

Twitter's *about page* gives us two other key pieces of intelligence.

1. 80 percent of Twitter users visit the site via mobile. That means every tweet you send needs to be mobile friendly, and every link you include in your tweets needs to look good on the small screen of a smartphone or iPhone.

2. 77 percent of Twitter users are outside of the United States which means there is a potentially huge communications gap. Many of the people who receive your tweets aren't going to understand what you're saying, so the visual element better tell your entire story. It if doesn't, you're wasting your time.

With that many tweets going out every day you can understand how easy it is to get lost in the clutter. Later in this section I'll give you some tips to cut through the noise, and make your tweets easier to find.

Twitter 101

Twitter is a form of microblogging.

Conversations on Twitter take place in real time and whittle the conversation down to short 140 character bursts.

The advantage to users is that it is instantaneous and occurs in real time. A lot of the breaking news stories you see on Headline News are broken on Twitter.

Here's the scenario. A lone gunman attacks a school or business. Trapped students capture footage on their cell phones and post it to Twitter. Moments later it's picked up by network news and spread across the media.

Another scenario that plays out every year during storm season is someone captures footage of a tornado roaring by their home as they're headed for the storm cellar. Minutes later the video hits Twitter, then it's uploaded to Facebook, the local news station's website, and next thing you know there's a viral video of the storm tossing a car into a tree or the house next door.

That's the instantaneous nature of Twitter. As soon as something happens you can have it online within seconds.

The good thing is disaster videos aren't the only ones that go viral. You can shoot a quick video of a dog chasing a note pinned to its tail, kids going crazy flinging mud or snowballs, or even of a staged accident or event at work.

The Least You Need to Know

You can open a personal or business Twitter account. There is very little difference between the two.

Next you need to edit your profile. A lot of businesses skip this step.

Big mistake!

At the very least you need to add your company name, contact info, links to your blog—website, or other social media accounts, a profile photo, and a short one line bio. Other than your contact info the most important stuff you enter here is your bio. It tells people who you are, why you're on Twitter, and how you can help them.

My author bio on Twitter is short, sweet, and says all you need to know about me—"Short easy to read solutions to your ecommerce problems."

My eBay Twitter bio takes the same approach—"Unique historical memorabilia covering the period from 1850 to 1970—magazine articles, newspapers, and vintage advertisements."

It's just 128 characters long, but gives readers a good idea of what I'm all about. Create your bio the same way. Twitter gives you 160 characters to introduce yourself, make an impression, and convince visitors to click on your links. Spend the time you need to craft an amazing bio.

Here's one other piece of advice. If you run a brick and mortar location as well as an eBay business focus on local. Let's say you're selling custom blended coffees in Seattle. Let people know you're located in Seattle. Depending on your business image make it snarky. "Unlike that other big name Seattle coffee shop, most coffee drinkers say our coffee packs a punch and doesn't drain your wallet." It's only 125 characters, but it tells your story, lets readers know you're not afraid to take on the big kid on the block, and hints that you won't have to ante up five bucks for a cup of java.

Overall, it gives readers a good impression of your business that may make them want to learn a little more about you.

Twitter also gives you an opportunity to upload a theme to help brand your page.

Twitter recommends 1500 x 500 pixels as the ideal size for your header, but you can upload any theme you like between the sizes of 1024 x 280 pixels and 2560 x 600 pixels. You can get all of the details by following this link. *http://ct-social.com/twitter-header-template-2014/*. You will also find a header template, and directions to help create an amazing header.

Getting Started

As I said earlier, tweets need to be short, sweet, and on target. You need to boil your message down to one quick point. That means you need to do a little planning before you start clicking the keys on your keyboard.

The first thing you need to do is select a tool to shorten the link you're going to use in your tweet. Two tools I recommend are **bitly** *https://bitly.com/shorten/* and **Google URL Shortener** *https://goo.gl/*.

Here's an eBay URL for an Otterbox iPhone 6 case.

http://www.ebay.com/itm/NEW-Otterbox-Defender-Commuter-Symmetry-Case-for-Apple-iPhone-6-Plus-5-5-/321639090877?pt=LH_DefaultDomain_0&var=&hash=item4ae3 2f0abd

Here's the same link after it's been run through **bitly**.

http://ebay.to/1xZQSsC

See the difference?

If you used the original link it's 156 characters. That's more than you're allowed for your entire tweet. After bitly performs its magic, your link is down to a svelte 23 characters. That leaves plenty of characters to craft an amazing tweet.

Here's an example.

Let's say you're running a big sale on iPhone 6 Otterbox cases this week, and you want to let potential buyers know about it. You could just blurt it out –

Large selection of iPhone 6 Otterbox Cases starting at $29.99 http://ebay.to/1xZQSsC

That's good. But, it doesn't really move anyone to take action.

What we need to do is rework it and use more action words that motivate readers to take action on your message.

Try this one on for size.

Refurbished iPhone 6 Otterbox case. Guaranteed to protect your iPhone. 2 days only. Starts at $29.99. Check them out. http://ebay.to/1xZQSsC

The entire tweet is just 139 characters, but it does everything you want it to. It tells potential buyers why (guaranteed to protect your iPhone), it includes a call to action (2 days only), and it gives the price (Starts at $29.99).

Not bad!

That's what you need to do with every tweet you send out.

1. Boil your message down to just the essentials.
2. Use action words wherever possible.
3. Include a call to action.

Here's another surprising factoid you need to consider. The shorter your tweet, the more likely it is to be read.

Research shows short tweets—between 80 to 100 characters are the most effective, and tend to get read the most. That means the less you say, the more effective your tweet is going to be.

Lesson learned.

K. I. S. S.

Keep it simple stupid!

#Hashtags# - The Art of Getting Found

Getting found on Twitter revolves around using hashtags—better known as the # sign.

If you want to boil Twitter SEO down to the bare bones—this is it. Hashtags are nothing more than searchable keywords. When you use a hashtag it makes it easier for other Twitter users to find your content.

Here are a few examples of hashtags commonly used on Twitter.

- #CocaCola
- #MylieCyrus
- #ValentinesDay
- #WorldSeries
- #iPhone6
- #SuperBowlChampions

As you can see, hashtags are nothing more than keywords proceeded by the # sign. Sometimes users include more than one hashtag in a tweet: #Beatles #John #Paul #George #Ringo. You're not breaking any Twitter rules by using multiple hashtags, but I'd suggest keeping it to no more than two. Anymore, and readers are going to think you're screaming for attention, or suffering from a bad case of keyword spamming syndrome.

Now that you know what hashtags are, let's take a look at how to use them.

The first thing to remember is you only want to use hashtags that are relevant to your business. Miley Cyrus is popular, and tweeting about her will get your tweet a lot of views, but if it puts the wrong eyes on your tweets it's not going to do you any good.

Let's take my eBay business for example. At first glance old magazine articles aren't sexy, or at the top of Twitter's trending list. But, if I position them correctly—they are relevant to a certain segment of the Twitterverse.

Try these tweets on for size, and pay special attention to the hashtags.

- Vintage magazine cover #MartinLutherKing assassination. Only one available.

- Original newspaper #AbrahamLincoln inauguration. Last day, bid now.

- Indian account of #CustersLastStand. Originally published in 1898. Make it yours.

- #VintageMoviePoster #GoneWithTheWind. One of kind collectible. Bid now.

- #HistoricalCollectibles #IowaHistory #AmanaColonies Largest selection anywhere.

Most of my posts follow the rule of one hashtag per tweet, but every now and then I break the rule because my content appeals to several different market segments.

Another thing you will notice is most of my hashtags come in the center of the tweet, rather than at the beginning. It's counterintuitive to what you'd think, but recent research shows placing the hashtag in the center of the tweet is more effective. I'm not sure why, but it seems to work. Test it for yourself to see if it boosts your response rate.

Several of my tweets also include a call to action—"Bid now." "Only one available." "Make it yours." "Last day." They're subtle hints that let readers know, you better act now, because this offer isn't going to last long.

Other businesses create a unique hashtag for their business name. It can be as simple as your name - #MoneyBagsPayDayLoans, or it can be a slogan - #BatteriesForLess. It may be a tag to help people discover your local business #QuadCityMagician or #DavenportDJ.

Whatever you decide for your hashtag strategy the key is to make it relevant. Choose hashtags that will help your business get discovered. If you're unsure whether a hashtag is a good fit for your business or not, run a search on Twitter and see what pops up.

Get Followed – How to Build Your Tribe

There's a lot of advice floating around about how to build your follower base. Some of it is good, some of it not so good. The reason I say this is a lot of the *gurus* endorse the more is better syndrome. Paris Hilton has ten trillion followers so you need to get that many too.

That's not quite true.

Sean Platt, Johnny B. Truant, and David Wright put it best in their book, **Write. Publish. Repeat**. To be successful you only need one thousand true fans. Their book is about building your career as an author, but the advice applies to any business trying to build a social media platform or fan base.

It doesn't take a bazillion followers to build your business. It just takes one thousand *true fans* who will buy every new product you release, and tell their friends.

Contrast this with the typical advice you're going to find about building followers on Twitter.

Here's the way it goes.

Make a list of the big players in your field. Start following their followers. If after two days they don't follow you back, unfollow them. Rinse and repeat. Over time you will amass a large list of followers.

Don't get me wrong. It's an effective strategy, and it has worked well for businesses that want to develop a massive number of followers. But, if you're a business, it's not about the number of followers you have, it's about the number of followers who will become customers and take action on your tweets.

Don't work harder than you have to.

Post eight to ten solid tweets a week. Offer valuable content that your followers will enjoy and use. Keep the amount of self-promotion to a minimum. For every ten tweets you shoot out, no more than one or two should be salesy. If you're followers get even the slightest hint you're more interested in selling to them than sharing with them they're going to unfollow you.

The key to success on Twitter is to provide great content that encourages readers to check out your bio and contact links. If you continue to provide pertinent content the sales will follow.

I know this has been said before, but social media marketing is more of a marathon than a sprint. Short bursts will get you attention, but staying in the game over the long haul is how you win.

Pinterest

Pinterest is nothing more than a ginormous virtual bulletin board. Users find things they like, and pin them on their board. After they've done that the magic starts. Other users stumble across their pins, and can re-pin them on their boards eventually sharing them with thousands of online viewers around the world.

Another way to think of Pinterest is to look at it as a virtual scrapbook where you can store (pin) all of your favorite things. The cool part is you don't need scissors, paste, or tape to put it together. Just click your mouse and your content is stored away, and ready for friends and strangers to check it all out.

Pinterest is actually a number of applications packed into one. It is a –

1. Social media site
2. A spot to bookmark all of your favorites
3. A content curation tool

The really exciting thing about Pinterest though, is it was designed to be more visually oriented right out of the box. That gives it a huge advantage over Facebook and Twitter. Unlike Zuckerberg and Company Pinterest doesn't have to retrofit their site to catch up. Instead they're forcing the big guns like Facebook to reengineer their timeline to make it more visually oriented.

The other thing Pinterest has going for it compared to other social media sites is it works.

I have hundreds of bookmarks I pinned on three Pinterest boards over two years ago, and they are still being re-pinned fifteen to twenty times per week. Try to get that kind of traction with Facebook or Twitter. It's not going to happen. Most posts made on those sites have a shelf life of a few hours to a few days.

The Least You Need to Know

When you sign up Pinterest shows a prompt where you can register as a business user, rather than as an individual. The easiest way to brand your business on Pinterest is to fill out your about section as completely as possible.

Use your business email address when you sign up. Choose the business type closest to your own. A little farther on down the page you get the opportunity to set up your business profile. If it's not already taken by another user select your business name. If it's not available try to pick something similar to it or another name that people associate with your business. Include your contact name if you would like visitors to your boards to know who you are.

There is also a spot for a picture. You can use your logo, or a shot of one of your products, but a better choice would be a picture of yourself. It will help visitors connect with you.

Below this you will see a section labeled *about you*. It gives your 160 characters to tell visitors all about you, and why they should do business with you. Again, don't sell. Use appropriate keywords that compel viewers to find out more about you. "Featuring historical collectibles from 1806 to 1970—magazines, newspapers, and historical prints." Or, "Custom presentation folders designed to wow your clients—guaranteed to increase your business."

If you're a local business that people can visit include your city, state, or region, whichever is more beneficial to your business. You're also able to add a website URL. If you don't have a website, copy and paste the link for your eBay or Amazon store.

Towards the bottom of this section you can include links to your various social media sites—Facebook, Twitter, Google+, and your Yahoo and Gmail accounts.

Getting Started

Getting started on Pinterest is about as easy as it gets. From the home screen click the plus sign in the box where it says *create board*. The board setup screen pops up next. First, it asks you to name your board. The skies the limit when it comes to names, but you can get a bigger bang for your buck if you use strong keywords in your board's name. If your board is about early American magazines, you could name it "Illustrated History or Early American Magazines from 1857 to 1899."

If it's a board detailing Theodore Roosevelt in the Spanish American War you could name it, "Theodore Roosevelt in the Spanish American War—San Juan Hill, Rough Riders." Doing it this way gives viewers three more opportunities to find it than just saying "Theodore Roosevelt" or the "Spanish American War."

Next up is the description box. You have 160 characters to tell everyone what your board is about. Be clear, concise, and load it with appropriate keywords. After this you need to choose a category for your board. Pick the one that is closet to your topic.

I've Created My First Board, Now What?

Congratulations! You created your first board, now what do you do?

That's a situation most users face every time they start a new board. What it really comes down to is what you expect to accomplish with your board. Do you want to get a ton of new followers? Do you want to drive traffic to your website? Or is your goal to direct people to your eBay store?

Give this Question some thought before you start pinning, because certain types of pins will create certain types of reactions on the part of your viewers. If you sell cellular phone accessories on eBay the ultimate goal is probably to drive traffic to your eBay store, but if all you post is links to items you have for sale, it's going to scare people away. They're going to think you're being to salesy. You need to take a more balanced approach. For every one or two store items you pin to your board, pin eight to ten links to stories about new phones and products.

The idea is to give visitors a wide variety of information centered around products they enjoy. Pin technical articles about how to reset their email, or product recall notifications. If you have your own blog or website, that's even better. Send viewers to content you've written, that way they're more likely to stumble across links to your eBay store, mail list, and other items you're selling.

The main thing is to stay focused. Don't pin pictures of your kids or your pets, no matter how cute you think they are. Your board is about your business and for it to do its job you need to keep your content focused.

When you pin items make sure you write a strong keyword loaded description. Also, when you're posting pictures or videos make sure you link to the source article or page so viewers can hyperlink to the original source.

Optimal picture size on Pinterest is 500 pixels wide x 600 pixels high. And, keep in mind taller pictures display better, so whenever possible try to post taller images.

Keep in mind you're not limited to just posting pictures or links, you can also pin videos from YouTube, Vimeo, and other streaming sites. If you're having trouble getting your stuff re-pinned video will set your boards on fire.

Here are a few other tips to help make your pins more effective.

1. You can add a price to your pins by adding a dollar sign or pound sign in the description. When you do this Pinterest will display the price in the upper left corner of your pin.

2. Pinterest is similar to Twitter in that you can use hashtags to make items more searchable. Again, don't go overboard with your hashtags—using #yummy or #wow won't help your pins get found.

3. If you have a website or blog you can add the Pin-it button to make it easier for users to share your content.

4. Don't use just one board. Create a number of different boards keyed to different user interests. That way your pins can be more focused, and more effective.

5. Female users outnumber male users by almost four to one so use soft colors, tone down your language, and post pictures and videos directed towards women.

YouTube

Video will set your eBay business apart more than any other thing you do because no one is doing it.

They're scared.

They don't understand it. So they don't do it.

That spells opportunity for you and me.

Here's the low down: *Adults aged eighteen to thirty-four tune into YouTube more than they do any single cable television network. YouTube is the place millennials go for digital content.*

More than one billion visitors flock to YouTube every day. Three hundred hours of video are uploaded to YouTube every minute. Sixty percent of your viewers will come from outside of your home country. And, more than half of YouTube views are mobile.

If you still have doubts about whether you should be doing video on YouTube consider this. YouTube is the third most visited website in the world, and the second most used search engine. And, since YouTube is owned by Google videos posted there rank high in Google search.

How to Use YouTube

1. Include a short video in each of your listings that introduces your business, and tells potential customers more about you, your products, and how you do business. Checkout Fiverr celebrity Professor Puppet as he introduces my eBay business—history-bytes. *https://www.youtube.com/watch?v=tVt6YlF_4hw.*

2. Create short how-to guides that show how to use the products you're selling, how to hook it up, or how to maintain it. Here's a link to a short video showing how to install the Otterbox Defender case on the iPhone 6. *https://www.youtube.com/watch?v=hjl5NkrbgiE.*

3. Review the products you're selling. Tell viewers what you like about the product, why you like it, what you don't like, and how it stacks up against the competition. When you do this, make sure you place the video on YouTube and in your product listing on eBay.

4. Share industry news. If you sell food service equipment and you just spent the week at NACS, or another regional show let viewers know about the awesome new ovens or food products you saw. Snag an interview with company reps or show officials. Every time you do this it will build your authority as an expert in your field.

What to Do in Your Video

Think of YouTube as a personal invite into a viewer's home. When they choose to watch your video they're inviting you into their home for a personal chat.

Make the most of it.

Use this opportunity to share your knowledge. Even if you don't think of yourself as an expert; chances are you know more than ninety percent of the people who are going to watch your video.

Be yourself.

Approach it like you're talking to a friend. If you're filming an introduction to your business the easiest way to do it is to sit at a table surrounded by some of the products you sell.

Introduce your business.

Tell people how long you've been in business, what got you started, and why you're so passionate about it. Point to a few of your products, or pick them up and show viewers what's so great about them.

Chances are after the first ten or fifteen seconds the nervousness will go away, and you will catch yourself thinking, "Why was I ever scared of this?" I know that's the way I felt after filming my first video book review for Amazon. I'd been planning to do it for a year but always found an excuse to put it off. Once I finished the first one I realized it was a cakewalk—just point the camera, and start talking.

Here are three tips to keep in mind when making your video.

1. Don't try to sell from your video. Focus on providing great content. If it's what people want, they will checkout your links and visit your eBay store, email sign up form, or social media sites.

2. Be consistent. Focus on a single topic—old books, baseball cards, GI Joe, Manga, or Anime. It's easier to build an audience when your content focuses around one topic. If you try to cover too many topics, viewers will become confused and look for more content elsewhere.

3. Keep it conversational. The best videos are relaxed—just you chatting with friends.

Necessary Equipment

Chances are you already have all of the equipment needed to get started posting YouTube videos.

Your smartphone or iPhone camera can capture higher resolution video than a high end camcorder from several years ago. If you have an iPad or other tablet, most models come equipped with one or two high resolution video cameras. Barring that many YouTubers open up their laptop and shoot video directly from the built-in video camera.

Sound is the major stumbling block when using any of these devices. The internal microphones often sound hollow, drop sound, or pickup background noise.

Most experts agree sound is the key to a good video. Because of the limitations imposed by built-in microphones most videographers suggest purchasing an external microphone. You can find good quality mics on eBay or Amazon for fifty to one hundred dollars.

One final word of advice on sound—be sure you have something to say. You don't have to script the whole video out. That's the surest way to chase viewers away if you just sit there and read a canned script. The best thing to do is jot down a few talking points, and glance down at them for help when you find yourself stumbling over what to say next.

Lighting is another key ingredient to making a great video.

I shot my first view video sitting in a recliner next to a table lamp. I just held my iPhone at arm's length and started talking. The end result was okay, but you could tell the lighting was off. Everything was sort of dark and shadowy.

There are a couple of ways to approach lighting.

The least expensive method is to film in areas where there is plenty of natural light. Outdoors is great in season. Barring that you can open the window shades and shoot your video in the open light.

If you have a little extra money to toss around you can set up an indoor studio. A desk or table surrounded by the products you sell makes an ideal background setting. You can pick up some flood lights or photography lights so you always have the proper lighting. That way you can film day or night with no worries.

The final piece of equipment you're going to need is an inexpensive tripod.

If you're shooting a short one or two minute video it's not too hard to hold your iPhone steady, but when your video starts to run five, ten minutes, or longer you're going to find it hard to hold your arm steady. And, wait until the first time you try holding a product in one hand and your iPhone in the other. Something has to give, and the odds are your hand is going to start shaking.

A tripod makes filming your video easier over the long haul. You don't have to worry about sudden movements in your video, and when you want to hold up a product or move around it's a whole lot easier when you're using a tripod.

In time you may want to dress things up a bit.

There is a lot of good video editing software available. *Windows Movie Maker* is free from Microsoft and relatively easy to use. There are several video editing apps available for the iPhone and Android phones. Just visit the apps store to check out what's available.

If you plan on making screen shots you can use *Camtasia* or *Snagit*. Another option is to use PowerPoint and post a slide show from it.

Shooting Your First Video

Don't worry that it's not perfect. Just do it. Everybody's first video looks like it was created by an amateur. It's okay. You will get better over time. Another thing you'll discover when you go back to look at your first videos six months or a year from now is they're not as bad as you thought. Here's a fact you might as well get used to: You're usually your own worst critic.

Here's a simple structure for your videos.

1. First 10 to 15 seconds. Say what you're going to do, and let viewers know why they should watch it.

    Here are a few quick ways to start your video.

    "This short video is going to cover the early history of Harper's Weekly Magazine from 1850 to 1876..." or "This short video is going to introduce you to the 1955 Topps Baseball card set, and help you recognize common grading problems."

2. 15 to 30 seconds. Tell them what's in it for them. "Harper's Weekly was published in one and two volume annual sets so it's important you know the details before making any purchase." "One of the problems with the 1955 Topps Baseball sets is scammers often trim the margins to make the card appear better than it is."

3. 60 to 180 seconds. Start talking. Deliver the information you promised in short easy bursts. Whenever possible

illustrate what you're talking about with stories and anecdotes.

4. 10 to 15 seconds. Recap what you talked about. Tell them what you talked about, why it's important, and what you want them to do next. Watch the next video in your series. Sign up for your email list, or check out your item on eBay.

Whatever you do, don't try to sell something directly from your video. YouTube lets you add links in your description below the video. If your video is good enough, viewers will check out your links. Some may even visit your listings—who knows, they may even buy something.

That brings us to setting up your video.

Your title and description determine how easily your video can be found in search. If you set things up properly you can focus thousands of extra eyes on your videos.

The title of your YouTube video serves the same purpose as the title of your eBay listing. It powers the site's search engine.

Keywords are king.

Your main keyword should be the first or second keyword in your title.

Example:

- Thomas Nast Santa Claus Illustrations in Harper's Weekly Magazine.
- Installing the Otterbox Defender Case on the iPhone 6
- 1954 Topps Baseball Inserts in Sports Illustrated Magazine

Another way to approach your title is to pose questions.

Example:

- Frequently Asked Questions About the 1955 Topps Baseball Card Set
- How to Grade Old Books and Magazines
- Why You Should Have Second Thoughts About Purchasing an iPhone on Craigslist

It's also important to sprinkle keywords throughout the description of your video. YouTube gives you 1,000 characters to craft your description so be sure you get it right.

Write naturally.

Your description should mirror your video. Tell viewers what it's about, why they need to watch it, what they will learn by watching it, and what you want them to do next. Include at least one link at the bottom of your description. It can be to your eBay store, your mail list signup form, or your social media sites.

The key is not to sell.

Provide links to your store, or wherever you have your items for sale. If your content is good enough viewers will make the next move and visit your store. You don't have to push them.

Tags help YouTube determine who to show your video to. Make sure to include the appropriate keywords in your tags. If you're in doubt about which ones to include check out your competition, and borrow from them.

And, here's one final tip.

Those in the know say Google transcribes videos to search for appropriate keywords so be sure to include your keywords in the context of your video.

Final Takeaway

To be effective you should provide several different types of videos. Nothing personal, but people are going to get tired of watching your videos if they're all of just you talking. To be effective you've got to shake things up now and then.

Here are some of the different types of video you should consider.

1. Talking head. Just like it sounds, you point the camera and people watch you talking from the shoulders up. It's the easiest type of video to make, and often the most effective if done right. Be yourself. Be natural. And, make sure the camera is adjusted properly so you don't chop the top of your head off.

2. Testimonials. Get some of your customers to hop in front of the camera and talk about the items you sell, or why they like doing business with you. Remember you can tell people and tell people how good you are, but it's more effective when someone else does the talking.

3. Screen capture. This is pretty easy stuff you can do a voiceover while you're capturing actions on the computer screen. Done properly these videos can be very effective, especially when you're doing computer tutorials.

4. Walk about. Take your camera and walk around your business. Introduce some of your key employees while they're doing their job. Catch someone asleep on the job, or goofing off. Maybe Dave and Sharon sing at break or when they're packaging shipments. There are several ways of doing this. Make it serious, or capture the goofy moments.

5. FAQs. Sit down at your desk and answer common questions about your business—shipping fees, combined shipments, returns, how items are packed, and how soon customers can expect to receive their order after hitting the buy button.

Interview with Lauren Lerner

    *I recently conducted an interview with Lauren Lerner of **Lauren's Fab Finds.** Lauren has been selling on eBay since 1999 and runs a high end women's fashion site on eBay. She is doing an amazing job of using email and social media marketing to power up her sales. The contents of this interview should prove enlightening to sellers who are struggling to grow their sales.*

    You can view Lauren's Fab Finds on eBay by following this link. http://stores.ebay.com/Laurens-Fab-Finds

. . . .

You're doing most of the things I talk about in this book: email marketing, Facebook, Pinterest, and You Tube. My first question is, how much time do you spend daily managing your social media activities? I know a lot of sellers who are going to say, "Sure, I'd like to do that, but who has the time?"

We spend quite a bit of time on social media. One of our staff handles the majority of it. He schedules almost all of our posts for the week. Some of the posts are scheduled through Hoot Suite so we can have them ready to go when needed. Others are posted in real time. Then there is time spent going through social media and responding to other peoples posts - like fashion bloggers, shopping experts, etc.

. . . .

What would you say to sellers who insist "That's too much work, especially when I don't know if it's going to pay off or not."

If you want to see an ROI on your social media efforts you need to put the time into this, just like you would spend the time to do a print media campaign or a media buy on television. You have to spend time thinking about what is your goal with social media and how can you achieve your goal. For some people it's just about putting up funny or cute posts....for other people it is about brand awareness....and for others it's about driving traffic to your website.

. . . .

There are so many choices out there: Facebook, Pinterest, or YouTube. Which channel works best for you, or do they all complement each other?

They do all complement each other. We are careful not to put the same exact content up on all three. Some things that we do are specific to each platform and we include Instagram and Twitter along with the three you listed. Facebook, YouTube and Twitter are three that get us the most engagement with our customers. Since our core customer base is women between the ages of 35 - 60, we focus on Facebook because that demographic uses Facebook the most.

....

You have a nice looking YouTube channel packed full of videos. Video is scary for a lot of folks, especially getting started. What would you recommend for someone just getting started with video?

Don't be scared. It's not live television. You can practice and get good at it. With today's technology all you need is a phone and simple editing software and you are all set. Start small with short commercials and then work yourself up to bigger things. However, keep your branding. If you are a high end retailer, your videos need to have that same look. It can't look like a kid made the video.

....

What types of video work best for you?

We do informational videos and sales video all the time. They work really well for us. When we are about to start a new sale, we will promote it with a video. Since we are an online store, the videos give our customers a real connection to me and some of my staff. They can see us and have a sense of what we are like because of the videos.

....

Do you script everything out, or do you just start the camera rolling and go at it?

The videos are definitely scripted. I have a staff member who writes, directs and produces all the videos. These videos are all thought out and planned very well. If you just ad-lib it, you will find that you are wasting a lot of time and the finished product will not look as good.

. . . .

I know I just started doing a lot of video reviews on Amazon, and the hardest part was getting started. I finally bit the bullet, fired up the camera on my iPhone, and started talking. I'm pretty sure I'd still be stalled out at the start zone if I'd kept trying to plan everything out. Is "just doing it" the best way to get started?

I would suggest having someone shoot the videos for you. If you want to practice your videos on your own, that is fine. But when it comes time to shoot the real thing, you want someone else to do it. Again, we are a high end fashion store, and our videos need to have that kind of feel to it. I can't do that by myself.

. . . .

I really like the cover page for your YouTube Channel. It's a perfect extension of your brand. Is that necessary to increasing your reach, or is it something that can wait until you grow your stock of videos?

This is all about branding. And our cover page is a part of it. When people come to our YouTube channel they know where they have landed. There is no reason to wait to put up the cover page. If you were a brick and mortar store, you would make sure your storefront sign was up before you had your grand opening.

....

I know from my own experience writing and marketing books, email is where it's at. Does email marketing drive your eBay sales? By that I mean, if you add a new product to your lineup, or run a sale with Mark Down Manager, do you find email marketing is an effective way to make more sales?

The eBay marketing newsletter really doesn't do well for us because there is no customization. We use Mail Chimp, and it helps remind our customers about sales and promotions. We rely on email marketing heavily to keep our name in front of our customers.

....

eBay is very protective of its customers, and takes a dim view of sellers contacting them to make off eBay sales. With that in mind, could you tell me a little about how you built your email list, and drove customers to your Facebook and Pinterest pages?

We build our list a few ways. First, there is a sign up form on our website. Second, every time we ship a package to a customer who bought something from our eBay store we include a professionally designed flyer. There is a QR code on the flyer that takes customers directly to our sign up form. Also, through all our social media campaigns, when someone engages with us on Facebook, Twitter, Instagram or Pinterest there are opportunities to sign up for the newsletter. There are also posts that we usually do once a week to promote signing up for our newsletters.

....

Let's say I'm a seller just starting out with email marketing. What kind of stuff do I send to my email list? Do I tell them about all of the great things I have for sale, or is it better to send them general information relating to the products I sell? I know with book marketing, we figure you should send one sales message for every ten information pieces. Are the rules the same for marketing your eBay business, or do you focus more on the items you have for sale?

With us, we focus 95% on sales. But we do that in different ways. The messages always vary. For example…

• Why pay retail, shop Lauren's Fab Finds and save 50% - 85% off retail stores

• Don't miss out on our newest listings including…

• Promoting a specific sale….

• Promoting rare and hard to find items that we are about to list to the general public…

• Sometimes we do market fashion tips as well…

....

eBay has a mailing list feature they use to send out regular emails to customers who subscribe to your list. If eBay is already contacting your customers, is it really necessary to do your own mailing?

And, I ask this for two reasons.

First, eBay's newsletters are pretty tacky. If you haven't seen them, it's probably because they're so forgettable. eBay's newsletters are just a group of links to some of the products you have for sale. They don't offer any information about your business, your brand, or what's going on in your niche.

Second, I don't know if you remember back in the day. Constant Contact provided an email newsletter service for eBay sellers. They sent a real newsletter to customers with articles that matched your customer's interests. What I liked was they tracked sales generated by their newsletters, and told you how many sales resulted from each issue. That way, there were no doubts whether email marketing worked, or not.

Do you find that your email newsletters tend to increase your sales?

We do use the eBay mail feature but get very limited, if any results. We use Mail Chimp for our newsletter because of the customization and list acquisition features.

....

There are laws that prohibit marketers from just putting customer names on your email list. That's why it's important to use a service like *Mail Chimp* or *A Weber*, because they take care of the legalities involved in opting customers in and out of your list.

With that in mind, what things did you do to get customers to join your mail list?

I mentioned how we acquire customers for our mailing list above. I do agree with you about the legalities. And that is one of the reasons that we use Mail Chimp.

....

Sellers have so many choices to promote their business these days: social media, email, and video. Do you think it's important to include social media in your eBay business, or is it just something to experiment with if you have some spare time?

I think social media, email and video are essential tools to grow your business. I wouldn't experiment with them.

I would make them a key part of your marketing strategy.

. . . .

Let's go back to email marketing. I know it's hard to put a dollar figure on your ROI from any kind of advertising, but after you've done it for a while, are you able to gage the effect a particular email campaign will have? Or is it more like sprinkling fairy dust, you put some out there and hope it will sprout wings and fly?

It is definitely not like fairy dust.

But that's not to say every email campaign gets a good ROI. Email marketing is a very inexpensive way to remind your customers about your sales, promotions or any other information that is relevant. Whether you use Mail Chimp, Constant Contact or any other email service, the cost is going to be a few hundred dollars at most.

If you are just starting out, and don't have a very large database, there are even free services. It's mostly your time that is biggest "expense."

We plan out our email campaigns every 3 months and adjust accordingly based on how sales are going and if we have any last minute promotions. We track data for every one of our email campaigns. I know how many people opened the email, which specific links were clicked and which forms were filled out. If there is an offer to buy something, I can also track how many sales were generated from the campaign.

. . . .

Most eBay sellers have no idea what email marketing is about let alone how to get started. What types of emails would you suggest they send out for their first campaigns? I know you say you have a sales goal or message you try to spread for most of your mailings.

How important is it for sellers new to email to plan their email campaigns before shooting them out to customer's email boxes?

For a first campaign you could do a "Sign Up for our Newsletter and Receive a Discount." Refer a Friend and Save." Or you could do something where you give good information to your customers. For us it could be "Top 10 Spring Fashions."

It is crucial to have plan for email marketing.

You don't want to do it too much or too little. And you also want your emails to complement your other marketing strategies like social media post, etc. Everything should be planned out to complement each other.

. . . .

Let's say my time is limited and I only have time to post on one or two social media sites? How do I decide which ones will give me the biggest bang for my buck, or for the time I invest.

Great question! It really depends on your audience, so you need to do some market research. Our customers are mainly women between the ages of 35 - 55. They are primarily on Facebook, and that is why we focus on them. If we were selling to teenagers, we would focus more on Instagram. So you can't really paint a broad brush and say that Facebook should be everyone's first priority. We go Facebook first, and Twitter second.

. . . .

All of your marketing communications have the same basic look and feel to them. When I visit your website, eBay store, Pinterest or Facebook page, I recognize right off that they are part of Lauren's Fab Finds. How important is it that sellers retain that consistent look and feel in everything they do?

Branding is extremely important for any company. We want a client to see us on any platform and know they are looking at Lauren's Fab Finds. Think about a major retailer like Coke. Their image is the same whether it is on TV, Billboards, Print Ads, Internet, etc. The same goes for an eBay business.

. . . .

Let's say I only have time for one social media platform. Which one would you suggest? Email marketing – Facebook – Pinterest – Instagram – YouTube?

If it was only one it would be Email Marketing.

Grow your list and send relevant information to your subscribers. On social media, you never know if it is being seen. With email marketing at least you know it is being delivered. If you consistently send your subscribers timely and relevant information, your emails will have a good open rate.

. . . .

Last year eBay released their own spin on social media – collections, followers, etc. What is your take on them? Are they important to sellers, or just another time suck sellers should steer clear of?

It is not really relevant to us. We list items that our customers want at prices they want to pay. That is what is going to make them come back and be repeat buyers. It is a nice feature that eBay offers but we don't spend time on it.

. . . .

Store owners have the ability to discount select items using Mark Down Manager, and the Promotions Manager that allows them to issue coupons, offer free shipping, or provide discounts for multiple purchases. What's your take on these tools? How have they worked for you?

These are ok for us. We use them, but don't rely on them too heavily. Again, I will go back to email marketing. If I use the Mark Down Manager to try to generate sales, and at the same time do an email marketing campaign, the ROI on the email campaign will be about 10X higher.

. . . .

Is there anything else you think readers should know?

Don't look at your business as "just an eBay business". Think of your business as an online retailer. Your advertising and marketing efforts need to be relevant to your customers, with the same branding and you have to use multiple platforms.

Interview with Cameron Loughlin

I recently conducted an interview with Cameron Loughlin, owner of Tempest Leather. He markets custom guitar straps (guaranteed for life) on his own website and on Amazon, and has been an eBay seller in a past life. Cameron has some good tips on using social media marketing that eBay sellers should find relevant.

You're doing most of the things I talk about in this book: email marketing, Facebook, Pinterest, and You Tube. My first question is, how much time do you spend daily managing your social media activities? I know a lot of sellers who are going to say, "Sure, I'd like to do that, but who has the time?"

I only spend about half an hour a day managing social media and most of is it is spent on Facebook. Facebook allows me to schedule posts ahead of time, so I'll spend a Saturday morning planning a sale for Monday and then I'll fine tune it on Sunday.

Consistency is the key to standing out in the minds of your customers. Update it as much as you realistically can, but remember that **it's a long game** *and ultimately it's better to have longevity and post a little then to post all the time and burn out after a year. I think a ton of businesses burn out because they aren't willing to stick with it over many years. My suggestion is to carve out an hour a week to start and just start posting pictures, articles and even giveaways if you have a product/service ready to go.*

. . . .

What would you say to sellers who insist "That's too much work, especially when I don't know if it's going to pay off, or not."

I would tell them to remember that most successful businesses win with the marathon approach not the sprint.

If you do a little every week, and sustain it for years you'll develop trust with you customers and you'll make new ones through word of mouth. The key is constantly getting better and knowing that it won't all happen at once. Hard work tends to be rewarded over time, but you have to love what you do to stick with it. Also, I would tell them that any kind of positive results from a social media campaign early on can really inspire because you it fires you up to keep going.

. . . .

There are so many choices out there: Facebook, Pinterest, or YouTube. Which channel works best for you, or do they all complement each other?

Facebook is the best by far for me.

It's simply the most interactive and fun. People are constantly logged into Facebook, and they are reading their newsfeed all the time. It's so easy to take a picture of your product or service and then put together a post. I actually have my Facebook account linked to my Twitter account so my updates occur simultaneously on both platforms. In this sense they complement each other well. **Side note:** *Running Facebook ads can get you many "likes" but might not get you an immediate ROI, so you need to think about it how it fits into your budget at first.*

. . . .

You mention that you have a YouTube channel. Video is scary for a lot of folks, especially getting started. What would you recommend for someone just getting started with video?

Great question. Create something of high value that your customers need.

1.   What is the question that your customers are asking themselves when they buy your product or service?
2.   How can you help them?

In our case I created a video on how to assemble a guitar strap, and now it almost has 1,000 views. Put yourself in the customers' shoes and go from there. What is frustrating to your customer, and how can you solve their problem?

. . . .

Do you script everything out, or do you just start the camera rolling and go at it?

I will write down bullet points that I refer to. I do multiple takes and then I take breaks and get back at it later in the day. I find that my speaking ability improves over the course of the day, and I become clearer on the topic.

. . . .

I know I just started doing a lot of video reviews on Amazon, and the hardest part for me was getting started. I finally bit the bullet, fired up the camera on my iPhone, and started talking. I'm pretty sure I'd still be stalled out at the start zone if I'd kept trying to plan everything out. Is "just doing it" the best way to get started?

Yes, and don't underestimate the power of having small success early on and just getting *something* out there. Any kind of positive reaction or sale will help you keep going. It's amazing how fired up I got over even one sale in the beginning.

Try to get it out quickly, because then you can get feedback and learn how to improve before you develop a full product or service line. The quicker you can fire up the iPhone or iMac camera to make a video the better.

. . . .

eBay is very protective of its customers. They take a dim view of sellers contacting customers to make off eBay sales. With that in mind, could you tell me a little about how you built your email list, and drove customers to your Facebook and Pinterest pages?

I would recommend using online giveaway software such as gleam.io to collect email addresses. This is a great way to ethically market to people. You can utilize this software through Facebook.

. . . .

Let's go back to Pinterest. It's such a visual site. I know I have several boards there. I pinned pictures of my books and blog posts and they get repined every day.

What's your experience with Pinterest? What type of stuff works best for you, and more importantly are you seeing results from it?

Pinterest is a nice passive platform for our company. I looked on Pinterest the other day and noticed my product was pinned many times, and I never did anything to promote it on Pinterest. But people saw my website, my Etsy site, and Amazon products, and then they pinned pictures of our guitar straps to Pinterest.

Pinterest is a nice platform in this sense but I haven't invested much time and energy into it directly. I'm glad it's there because it helps drive traffic to our site when people see our pins!

. . . .

How important is it that sellers retain that consistent look and feel in everything they do? Should all of your social media sites, your website, and eBay store have the same look and feel to them?

Consistent branding is an important characteristic that ties your message together. When you're very consistent it clarifies the message you're sending out. There are millions of marketing messages going out every week and by having a concise, uniform message you can get people's attention.

. . . .

Let's say I only have time for one social media platform. Which one would you suggest? Email marketing – Facebook – Pinterest – Instagram – YouTube?

Facebook—all the way. It's more dynamic than the other platforms, and a great way to interact with your customers. It's very easy to run advertisements to drive impressions, clicks, and even sales.

. . . .

Is there anything else you think readers should know?

I think the key is sticking with whatever you do from a marketing standpoint. Occasionally a business will see a post go viral and blow up, but most of the time it's a slow process that takes a while.

Don't give up and do a little every day!

Blogging

A good blog can set you apart as an expert in your field, and drive buyers back to your eBay listings. A bad blog can drive potential buyers away just as fast.

What's the difference?

It's what you put in your blog. A lot of eBay sellers set up what I like to call splogs (spam blogs). You've probably bumped heads with several of these bloggers. They like to list the items they're selling in every blog post. They do the same thing on Facebook and Twitter.

Guess what?

Nobody wants to look at that stuff. They want to check out content related to the items you're selling. They want to hear the inside story about how their favorite collectibles were made, how to take care of them and store them safely, and about the guy who discovered a rare early baseball card set while cleaning out his neighbor's barn. If you're selling high end fashions, they want to see info on designers, fabrics, and new lines that are in the works. If you're fortunate enough to score an interview with a top designer you'll bring tons of new readers to your blog and most likely focus hundreds of new eyes on your eBay store.

The key is to provide content focused on what you sell. Concentrate on what interests your customers and they will find you, you won't have to worry about finding them.

What I do is put an about me page on my blog. It includes a short bio that tells readers about me, what I do, and how I got started selling on this crazy website called eBay. At the bottom of my bio readers can find links to my eBay and Amazon stores. It's a subtle sell, but it works. My about me page receives hundreds of hits every month, because readers want to know more about who's providing them with the blog info, and how reliable it is. When it comes down to it they want to know if they can trust me and the information I'm providing them.

I provide something the sploggers don't—the story behind what I sell. It helps position me as an expert in the historical collectible field. Who wouldn't feel good buying from an expert?

And, do you know what? I never have to ask readers to check out my eBay store. They discover the links for themselves when they visit my about me page.

What Kind of Content Should You Provide?

Content is king on your blog.

You need to consistently provide great content that educates, informs, and entertains your audience. If your content is bad, it doesn't matter how many readers you draw to your blog, they won't bookmark your site and return for another serving.

With that said what kind of content should you provide?

Here is a short list of the types of posts you should try to provide:

1) **Lists**. People go goo-goo ga-ga over lists. These are some of the most popular blog posts you can write. It can be as simple as a list of the top ten ways to save money on Wi-Fi, or twenty-five ways to lose stubborn belly fat.

There's something about a list that makes people want to take a peek and see what they're missing. Hint: Include a number in the title and readership will triple. I don't know what it is, but including a number in your title reels people in.

2) **Short informational posts**. These are some of the easiest posts you will write. They should be somewhere between 300 to 500 words and focused on a single topic. Make it informative, but light and easy to read.

You should write three or four of these posts every month. They're a quick easy way for you to connect with your audience.

3) **Wrap up or overview post**. In a wrap up post you pick a topic, and curate content on it. If I was publishing a celebrity blog, I might write a post about celebrity baby bumps. I could do a review piece, highlighting content that has been hosted on other blogs or news magazines in the past week, month, or whatever period I am looking at.

This post is going to take a little longer to put together because you need to go out and gather links, and then write a short article that ties them all-together. Review posts offer an easy way to add video to your blog. Search You-Tube for related videos, write a short comment tying it into your post, and embed the video.

Depending upon your subject you can do one of these posts every week, every two weeks, or every month. It's the type of post people will keep coming back for if you can provide them with good useful links.

4) **Tell a story**. Everybody loves to hear a good story. At least once a month you should share a story with your audience. It doesn't have to be long, 250 to 500 words is fine. It can be about something that happened to you, about a historical event, or something happening in the news. Be sure to keep it light and entertaining.

5) **Informational post**. These are the pillar of your blog. They offer an in depth look at one particular aspect of your topic. These posts can run anywhere between 1500 to 3500 words depending upon the subject.

For these posts to be effective they need to contain a lot of unique and useful information. They should contain links to outside sources, videos, and other people's blogs.

The easiest way to discover a relevant topic is to Google "hot topics in *****." The search results should return things your audience is interested in right now. Pick one, and give your audience the answers they need to form an opinion.

6) **Interview someone in your field**. One of the easiest ways to become an authority figure is to be seen in the company of people who already have that authority. Interviewing a celebrity or authority figure is a great way to piggy back off of their fame.

Getting started is easier than you think. If you want to interview another blogger, check out their contact page and drop them an email. Keep it short and to the point. Give them a link to your blog, and explain what you want to do.

You can do the same thing with the author of a book concerning your blog topic. Contact the author, and let them know you are looking at reviewing their book, and you would like to include a sidebar about them. Most authors will be glad to answer a few questions, and even supply a current photo you can publish with the interview. Make it a win – win for both of you.

Whenever I've been interviewed or conducted an interview, we normally swap questions and answers by email, and follow up with a short phone call to answer any lingering questions the interviewer might have.

7) **How to post**. People love how to posts. They can be as short as one hundred words, or as long as several thousand words depending upon what you are trying to explain.

How to posts offer an excellent opportunity to add video, especially if it's a hand's on project. Let me give you an example: My wife broke the "H" key on her computer. She purchased the repair kit online for $7.00, but didn't know how to install it. Along comes YouTube to the rescue with a detailed video showing how to replace a computer key.

You could create your own videos, or you can find a series of videos on YouTube and present links to them to help solve your reader's problems.

Set Up a Posting Schedule

Search engines love websites that consistently add new and unique content. The more often you add content, the more often they will send their spiders out to search for it.

As a new blogger your first goal should be to post ten or fifteen great articles as quickly as possible. Content is the most important thing at this point. You want to have enough articles on your blog to convince your audience you can deliver the info they want.

Once you've posted your initial articles it's time to develop a regular blogging schedule.

One or two posts a week is fine starting out, especially if you are delivering solid content. Shake them up a bit. Offer some informational posts, some short posts, a how to, an interview, and a wrap up. People come in different flavors, and you can never be sure which type of post they will find more enjoyable.

Select a Blog Platform

There are a lot of blogging platforms available: Blogger, Word Press, Tumblr, and Typepad. Any of them will work for your new blog.

The two most popular options are Blogger and Word Press. They offer more flexibility and control over your blog.

Personally, I prefer Blogger. It's easy to use. It offers a good variety of themes and layouts, and it's easy to customize. You have the option of assigning a custom URL to your blog, which gives it a more professional look and feel.

Other people swear by Word Press. It offers more features than Blogger; is served up on an independent platform, so you have total control over your blog; has thousands of pre-made themes you can download and apply to your blog; and it allows you to use a custom URL.

The choice ultimately comes down to which you prefer. Either one will do a great job for you.

Track Your Followers

To know where you're going, you need to know where you've been.

Blogging is sort of like taking a trip. When we were kids we always watched the odometer to figure out how far we traveled on a vacation. A statistical tracker does the same thing for your blog; it lets you see how much traffic your blog receives. What I like about blogger is it has a blog stats feature built into the control panel. I can tell at a glance what my top blog posts were for the day, week, or all time; where the traffic came from; what operating system readers used; and the keywords they searched on to bring them there.

For more detailed information you can install Google Analytics on your blog. It's easy to use. You just need to sign up for the service (It's free), and copy the tracking code into each of your posts. Google Analytics gives you awesome details about your website visitors, down to which pages they entered and exited your blog from, and how long they spent viewing each post.

My recommendation is to spend an hour every month reviewing your stats. It will give you some great insight into your visitors, and where they are spending their time on your blog. The answer might be totally different than what you expect. You never know until you check.

Final wrap up

Blogging is a fun way to reach out to like-minded people. It gives you the opportunity to position yourself as a product expert in your field. Just remember, be generous with the information you share, refrain from self-promotion and constant plugs for your eBay store. Provide amazing content, and readers will check out your about page, and some will even find their way to your eBay store.

Content is king. You need to provide a lot of unique entertaining content focused around the products in your eBay store.

Use Kickstarter to Fund and Grow Your Business

Most eBay businesses get started with little or no money out of pocket. Sellers begin by listing items they already have around the house. As time goes by they decide eBay is a pretty decent way to make a few extra bucks.

The next step may be to sell a few things for friends and neighbors. More often than not they check out a yard sale, garage sale, or local estate sale, and then see what's available at local thrift stores.

If these sellers need financing it normally comes from their personal credit card.

Up until now that's been the extent of financing available to eBay sellers. Banks aren't too obliging when they hear the words "eBay" and "business" used together. All too often negative connotations come to mind, and the banker ends up telling you it's "a great concept, but _____." (You can fill in the blank.)

Kabbage is another financing option available to eBay and Amazon sellers. Kabbage offers small business loans from $500 to $100,000 to online sellers based upon sales data from their eBay and Amazon accounts. Their finance rates aren't cheap. I think I paid $90.00 in interest and fees on a $500 loan. The good thing is you get the money quickly—most often within an hour or less of applying. It's deposited directly into your PayPal account, and payments are deducted from your PayPal account.

If you have a brick and mortar location or a connection with a local banker more options may open up to you, but for most sellers—the only choice is to use their personal credit card, or to get a short term loan from Kabbage.

. . . .

Crowdfunding is one of the newer financing options available.

At its most basic level crowdfunding is asking a group of like-minded persons to back you. In essence you tell them, I have this cool idea for a new way to sell Manga on eBay, but I need a little cash to get it started. In return for their support (money) you reward backers with different incentives. For $5.00 you may give them a shout out on your home page or a free digital download. For $25.00 you may offer them a first edition of a new Manga, for $250 you could offer them a hand-signed poster from a semi-famous artist, and for $2500 the reward could be an invitation to the online opening of your new store, or maybe you could offer to feature the backer's face somewhere in your store graphics.

The most successful crowdfunding campaign to date was the *Veronica Mars* Kickstarter in 2013. Producers raised nearly six million dollars from 91,000 backers who couldn't get enough of the TV series. $25 backers were rewarded with a digital download of the movie, $200 backers received a movie poster hand-signed by the cast, and one lucky $10,000 backer received a speaking role in the movie.

In effect crowdfunding is the coming together of people and an idea. It's a collaboration to make something happen.

For eBay sellers it's a tougher sell because in most cases you're raising money for a commercial product with just one purpose in mind—to make more money. So if you intend to attract backers, you need to craft one hell of a story.

The Least You Need to Know

The first thing you need to know about *Kickstarter https://www.kickstarter.com/* is you're either "all in" or you're "all out."

If you set your goal at $10,000, you don't get one cent if you don't raise at least $10,000. If you raise $9,999 you're out of luck. None of those credit cards get charged, and you walk away empty handed.

Think it can't happen to you?

More than 55 percent of the projects listed on Kickstarter don't reach their goal. The numbers are even gloomier when you look at all crowdfunding platforms—25 percent of all projects listed don't receive even one cent in backing.

How scary is that?

I'm not telling you this to discourage you from running a Kickstarter, rather I'm trying to help you understand how important it is to have a plan and thoroughly research your project before you get started.

The first thing you need to know about Kickstarter is it's not about getting money to fund your business. It's about getting money to fund a project.

So if you need to raise $100,000 so you can start selling iPhones on eBay, it's not going to happen. Not on Kickstarter anyway. If you're business makes custom cases for the iPhone 5 and 6 with custom graphics or a hot new design you created, Kickstarter just might be the ticket to help you launch your business.

The reason custom iPhone cases could get funded is it's a unique project. If you're graphics are cool enough, or if the design is unique and stands out head and shoulders over what's available on the market—it just may go viral, and grab the interest of backers.

Here's another example.

If you ask for $25,000 to start an online CD store, you're unlikely to attract any backers, except your mom and your Uncle Bob (and even they may be a hard sell). But, if you're the lead singer in a local or regional band and you run a Kickstarter to raise the cash to press your first CD to sell in your eBay store that could grab a whole lot of backers, as would a CD of local school kids singing regional folk songs or Christmas carols.

Do you see the difference?

A Kickstarter is something you use to launch a special one-time project, not to fund an ongoing business. That's not to say you can't fund a string of similar projects that turn into an entire product line for your eBay store. If you run a successful Kickstarter to fund a CD for a local band, there's nothing to stop you from running another Kickstarter for the same band's next album, or an entire run of albums for many local or regional bands.

It's all about breaking your goal down into a series of attainable projects.

Getting funded

What if you ran a Kickstarter and nobody came out to back you? It'd be sort of embarrassing, wouldn't it? Remember back to those statistics I gave you earlier—25 percent of all crowdfunding projects never receive one penny in backing, and 55 percent of Kickstarter's never launch.

Here's a tip I heard over and over again from successful and unsuccessful Kickstarter's. Ask for the smallest amount of money necessary to get your project off the ground. We all want a million dollars, but if ten thousand dollars will help your project achieve lift off, set your goal at ten thousand dollars. You may get a whole lot more, you may not, but if you hit $10,000 Kickstarter is going to run all of those credit cards, and ka-ching! You're in the money!

That's the great thing about Kickstarter. They don't shut the faucet off when you reach your goal. Some projects go on to raise five or ten times their initial goal. And, that's another thing successful Kickstarter's say, try to have enough momentum going into your project that you can meet your goal in the first three days. That way anything else you take in is just frosting on the cake.

What You Need to Know

1. Kickstarter reviews and vets all projects. Your odds of being approved are roughly 50 percent. If you've got a sustainable idea, but they think it needs a little work, the folks at Kickstarter will give you tips to make it more fundable.

2. You need to choose a time frame for your Kickstarter. It can be as short as one day, or as long as sixty days. Keep in mind—longer is not always better. Kickstarter says projects attract the most backers during their first three days and last three days, so it's those six days that make or break your project. The majority of sellers I've talked to say thirty days are the sweet spot, any longer and you encourage backers to procrastinate and possibly miss funding your project.

3. Remember, you're asking people to help you, but it's not going to work if you come right out and beg for help. Instead you have to show backers how your project can help other people, or help them. Make sure backers understand it's not about the cash; it's about being part of something new and exciting—like bringing back Veronica Mars.

4. Video is the key. A fancy video is nice, but it's more important to get out there in front of the camera and be yourself, be genuine, and explain your project in terms people can relate to.

5. One video isn't going to be enough. You need a series of videos. Create one or two videos that explain your project. Try to get a couple of your backers to talk about your project, and what excited or intrigued them about it. As your project progresses create several videos to update people on your status—"we're almost there." "We're so close, and every donation you make will bring us that much closer to hitting our goal." Or, "we just created a new stretch goal so be sure to check out our new reward levels, and what hitting our new goal will let us achieve."

6. Be sure to tell backers why it's important for them to help you. Let them know why you need their help, what's in it for them, and what will happen when you hit your goal. Remember, if backers don't understand why they need to contribute, your project isn't going to get off the ground.

7. Creative rewards are important to getting more backers and funding your project. You need several different levels of rewards to achieve liftoff. At the low end, you can give a shout out on your blog or website, or offer a digital download. The midrange--$25 to $50—is the perfect spot to offer a custom t-shirt, an autographed book or something with a higher perceived value. At the high end, over $100—you need unique rewards that

make backers feel they're part of something special, and that they're really helping to make it happen. The best way I heard it described was to decide what it's going to take to get someone to give up a latte, or dinner and a movie out, and help them justify why they should forgo some of life's little pleasures to back you instead.

8. Professional quality pictures are essential. You've got to show your project in its best light—up-close, with people using it if possible. Make sure your pictures and videos tell the story. Most backers are just going to look at your pictures, and make a decision based upon what they see. Others will decide from looking at pictures and videos whether they're going to read your text to get the rest of the story.

9. If things go totally wrong and you don't hit your goal, it's not the end of the world. Be a gracious loser. Email your backers and thank them for their support. If you lined up a different source of funding in the meantime, let backers know your project is going to move forward despite the setback on Kickstarter. Whatever you do, let your backers know what's next—a new Kickstarter, or maybe a scaled back version of your project.

10. Whether your project was funded or not, take time out to analyze your Kickstarter. What went well? Where did it all fall apart? It's not a total loss if you can learn from your mistakes. If no one backed your project you may need to approach it from a new angle, or you may decide it's time to move on and try something different. It may be that even though you didn't hit your goal you created

enough publicity that you can pick up commercial financing, or a new set of backers. Whatever you do, don't just throw in the towel without taking time to analyze what happened.

Kickstarter – The Nuts & Bolts

Setting up a Kickstarter is pretty straightforward. Navigate your way to *https://www.kickstarter.com/*. Click on *learn more*, and then *start a project*. Kickstarter will show you the following sentence—"I want to start a_____ project called _____." Fill in the two blanks, and you're ready to get started.

There are fifteen categories to choose from for your project type: arts, comics, crafts, dance, design, fashion, film and video, food, games, journalism, music, photography, publishing, technology, and theater.

The most successful categories are film and video, music, design, games, art, and publishing. What that means is if you choose a project that fits into one of these categories you are more likely to get funded.

Next you need to give your project a title. Don't try to be cutesy or clever, instead say what your project is about. If you're a local band, title it "Davenport, Iowa River Rats premier CD," or "Pictorial History of Black Hawk State Park."

After you enter you enter the title you will be taken to the product page. This is where all of the magic starts to come together. So before you begin make sure you understand what each step is asking you to do.

The first thing you're asked for is a project image. Keep in mind, this is the money shot. This is how people will judge your project. When potential backers see it, it has to grab their attention and entice them to keep scrolling down the page. Kickstarter recommends your picture should be at least 1024x768 pixels, and have a 4:3 aspect ratio.

Next you get a chance to revise your title. You've got sixty characters to work with so make them count. Don't mince words, or try and be clever. Your title needs to be clear, concise, and contain two or three keywords that tell people what your project is all about. Hint: Your title is searchable by keyword along with your name, so this is one of the ways people are going to find you. Make it easy for backers to find your Kickstarter and you will attract more donations.

The next space asks for a short blurb—just 135 characters. It needs to whet someone's appetite and make them want to keep scrolling down the page to discover what's next?

After this you pick a category and sub-category for your project. And, then you set your location. I think location is one of the key areas, especially if you have any kind of regional following. This is one of Kickstarter's real strengths. Backers can search through projects to locate Kickstarters in their hometown, state, or region, so you want to make sure they can key in on you.

After location, you need to pick a funding duration. That's just a fancy way of asking how long you want your Kickstarter to run. Thirty days is the suggested sweet spot, but you can make it as short as one day, or as long as 60 days. Just keep in mind what we talked about earlier—most backers pick up on a project in its first three days and its final three days. These are the days you need to be pushing the hardest.

The final thing you need to do in this section is set your funding goal. Remember, you may want $100,000, but if $10,000 will launch your project, that's the amount you should ask for. Kickstarter is an "all or nothing" environment, if you don't reach your funding goal, you don't get anything—no matter how much was pledged.

That's as far as I'm going to take you with setting up your Kickstarter. They have an awesome section to walk you through telling your story. You can access it by following this link *https://www.kickstarter.com/help/handbook/your_story*.

Getting the Word Out

So, you've created a Kickstarter now what?

Just about every person I talked with who created a Kickstarter offered the same advice. Running your campaign is a full time job. It requires planning, research, and constant getting out there 24 / 7 to share your story.

Here's one thing most people don't understand. Kickstarter is only going to bring you ten to fifteen percent of your backers. It's up to you find the other 85 percent of your funding. Sounds sort of like what I told you about eBay, doesn't it? Kickstarter is a platform to conduct your crowdfunding campaign on. Getting the word out is up to you.

Here the top ten tips I discovered to help you run a more successful Kickstarter.

1. Build your tribe before you get started. To be successful you need an email list, and a substantial Twitter and Facebook following. That way when you start your Kickstarter you can have them jump in and be your initial wave of backers.

2. You need to research other Kickstarter's in your category to see how they're approaching things. Learn from what they're doing right; eliminate the mistakes they're making.

3. Go local. If you're a local band, musician, writer, manufacturer whatever, reach out to the local media. Get as much publicity as you can. Submit press releases. Get on local TV and radio programs, and seek out opportunities for write ups in the newspapers and local magazines.

4. Reach out to niche bloggers. Offer to do interviews, guests posts, or provide free content for them. If possible work out a trade where you can do something for them if they email their list with details about your Kickstarter.

5. Ask family, friends, and work associates to help get the word out in their social networks. You never know, they may have the ear of an influencer who can help your Kickstarter go viral.

6. Rewards are important to your success. According to Kickstarter $25.00 is the most common backing, while $70.00 is the average backing. What that tells you is you need to focus a lot of sweet rewards in the $25.00 to $75.00 range. You don't have to break the bank, but give them a high perceived value—a special edition of a CD, book, or print, a hand signed t-shirt, or whatever you feel your audience will value more than the backing you are requesting.

7. Keep adding content to your Kickstarter page. Research shows many backers sneak two or three peeks at your story before they decide to back you. Be sure to add new content, especially more videos and pictures. Update your page to let backers know how close you are to reaching your goal or about new stretch goals and rewards if you've already reached your initial goal. The main thing is to keep backers in the loop.

8. Back a few projects before you post yours. It provides social proof that you play well with others, and Kickstarter has a spot at the top of each project page that shows how many projects you've backed. If that spot is blank, it makes you appear somewhat like Mr. Scrooge. You're looking for handouts, but you're not willing to help out. "Bah! Hum-bug, Mr. Scrooge!"

9. You need to show why you're the best person to complete the project you posted. Tell backers what's special about you. What makes you the right guy to get this thing done? Have you tackled a similar project? Share your motivation, so people will know you're the right guy or gal for the job.

10. You can lose, and still come out a winner. Just because you didn't get the funding you asked for doesn't make you a loser (it just means you'll have to try a little harder). A successful Kickstarter can generate a lot of publicity that will help grow your business down the line. It can be a great conversation starter. "We didn't get funded, but we got a lot of great responses." Or, "we learned…" It might provide the feedback you need to come back with an improved and even better product. I even talked with a gentleman who wasn't asking for money. Alan Fine's niche is ghost stories, and he created a website that asked backers to contribute ghost stories rather than cash. If you want to explore this option in more detail here is Alan Fine's webpage *http://www.catalystghoststories.com/#!no-cost-crowdfunding/c43i.*

Interview with Hanson Grant

(Hanson Grant recently ran a Kickstarter Campaign for a game he created. It's called Think Board. *That was in July of 2014. Grant raised over $10,000 to fund his project. Here's a link to his Kickstarter campaign https://www.kickstarter.com/projects/960330975/think-board-a-creative-space-for-endless-ideas)*

. . . .

According to Hanson the best resource he had was his group of supporters. Many of his friends were eager to help with the production of the video, including brainstorming, filming and editing.

Launching the campaign was a different story altogether. It required reaching out to friends who had a strong social media presence. Most of his marketing was done through Facebook and Twitter. The eventual payoff was huge—nearly 700 shares.

In the end, order fulfillment created the most difficult challenge. Luckily Hanson and his friends were up to the challenge, and he was able to get everything shipped.

According to Hanson the biggest lesson he learned was not to offer such a large variety of rewards. "I offered roughly 10 different rewards," he says, "which got confusing and difficult with a large number of backers. If I had any more than 300 backers I would have been far in over my head."

Hanson says the secret to his success "was the landing page, and the emails I sent. I set up a Landing Page for my website, which created a very easy way to share the campaign on Facebook and Twitter, and also watch and /or back the Kickstarter."

The second secret was "using Boomerang, which gave me the ability to craft over 300 emails, and have them timed to send at 8:01am, July 1st, the minute after the Campaign launched."

"Each email had a link to the Landing Page, and a request to share on their social media pages, or if they were feeling generous, back the product."

Hanson says he chose Kickstarter because he felt it was better known the general population, and had more of a "cool new product" feel.

Since the Kickstarter campaign, his company has been featured on WCVB TV - *The Chronicle* four times, in an article in *USA Today College*, and has received bulk orders from companies like Ernst and Young, Lockheed Martin, and Babson College.

And, get this—he's launching his next campaign soon!

. . . .

(Here's the entire text of the interview for readers who would like more insight on running their own Kickstarter campaign.)

Why did you choose Kickstarter for your crowdfunding campaign? There are a number of choices out there that aren't as strict. What made them more attractive?

I chose Kickstarter because I felt like it was a little more known by the general population, and had more of a "cool new product" feel. I also really enjoyed the all or nothing model, because it may have driven more attention, as a "let's do this together" campaign, instead of a "let me see how much I can get."

. . . .

I get what's in it for the person doing the Kickstarter campaign. What's harder for me to understand is what's in it for the guy who's backing you? What makes someone back a Kickstarter campaign? Is it the incentives you offer them at different levels, or is it just a need to be a part of something?

The number one reason for a backing is to back the entrepreneur. If the community believes in you, it's going to be a hit. If not, well, that's going to be a lot more work. Offering cool rewards is a nice way to show your gratitude for their support, but a lot of the time the video, entrepreneur and concept drive the support.

. . . .

How important are the incentives you give out for the different levels of contributions? I mean how attractive do you need to make those offers to conduct a successful crowdfunding campaign?

It's different with every campaign, but essentially, it has to be a little lower than what you would like to retail at. The backers are not customers. They do not know how credible the idea - product - entrepreneur is yet. Survey a few people to see what they would pay, and the set the price. Just be sure that after packaging, shipping, and labor, that you'll make the money you are looking for.

. . . .

Can you tell me a little bit about the incentives you offered to contribute? What did you offer? What was most effective? What do you wish you would have done different?

I offered multiple combinations of Think Board sizes - Some individual, some in packages with others. The most effective one is generally priced around $20. The one thing I wish I would have done differently, is offer fewer packages. If I kept it simple, and only had 3-5 backing offers, the fulfillment would have been 10 times easier.

. . . .

What's more effective as an incentive, especially at the higher level, a high dollar value item, or personalized coaching or a group meeting with your backers?

Personally, no one chose the group meeting. I think just a high dollar value item is the best. Offer a bulk deal in case anyone wants a large amount for his or her home/office. Let them know that it's an option to produce that many at this initial round of operations.

. . . .

Everything I've read about running a Kickstarter campaign says you need to approach it like a real job. And, by that I mean you need to have a plan for what you want to accomplish, and you need to be working at it constantly? You have to pump people up, keep them aware of your goals, and update them on how you're doing. Can you talk about this a little?

It's a commitment, it really is. While you may think once the campaign is up and running, the job is done, that's the farthest from true. I put in roughly 30 hours a week running this campaign. I opted out of working over the summer to give it my full-undivided attention. I couldn't imagine running a campaign while working 40 hours a week somewhere else. Also, if you don't commit the time now, when it's successful, how will you commit the time when it's needed most.

. . . .

How long did you run your Kickstarter campaign for? If you had it to do over, would you run if for more or less time?

30 Days. Statistically, 30 days is the best time to run a campaign because the backers see that you are committed to getting the project funded. If it is any longer, backers won't feel the urgency to back.

. . . .

It's essential to hit your goal with Kickstarter, because if you don't—you don't get any money. With that in mind, should you ask for less than you need, or do you ask for what you need and come out punching?

Come out punching. It's not as common as you'd think to get more money than your goal. Yes, some projects get 500% of their goal, but those are the ones you hear about. It's the ones you don't hear about that don't get funded, or barely make it.

. . . .

Going back to the last question, it's great to hit your goal, but the real money seems to be in exceeding your goal. I see a lot of campaigns that double or even triple their original goals. I've also noticed that they're out there constantly—on social media, on Kickstarter, and on their blogs and websites adding additional incentives if they hit this push goal or that threshold. How important is this to being really successful?

I wouldn't say it's crucial, but I do feel it is a benefit. My Kickstarter raised $100 over the goal, and to me that was enough. After Kickstarter came the real success, with TV interviews and write-ups on new sources such as USA Today.

. . . .

Kickstarter encourages everyone to upload a video. How important is that to your success? And, how creative does that need to be?

If you don't upload a video, it'll be hard to get support from the random Kickstarter people. It's your way to show who you are, so show them.

Most people, if they can't see it, they won't trust or believe in it.

. . . .

What do you think attracts backers to a Kickstarter campaign? Is it your project? Is it how you present it and how imaginative you are? I guess what I'm really asking is—is there some kind of magic sauce you can sprinkle on your Kickstarter campaign that will virtually guarantee success, or is it a crapshoot?

A very organized and user-oriented page will drive vitality. Those who drive crazy results, have a clean video, supporting videos in the descriptions, and a very transparent description of how everything works.

. . . .

A lot of the people I've talked with had trouble gaining traction outside of their circle of friends which limited the backing they received. What was your experience?

Actually, 75% of the backers were unknown. I think the reason for this was because of the shares on Facebook. I think it helped build up the business for after the Kickstarter too, instead of just raising money.

. . . .

Last question, I promise? If you could only give someone getting ready to start their Kickstarter journey one piece of advice, what would it be?

After the video, launch and campaign, upload all of your CSV files into PayPal Multi-Order Shipping. In there, you can create all of the shipping labels in seconds.

Interview with Brandon Kelly

(Most of the stories we hear about Kickstarter are from businesses that knocked the ball out of the field, and doubled or tripled their initial goal. In this episode Brandon Kelly, CEO NYCVanity - home of The Palit talks about her failed Kickstarter campaign and some of the lessons learned from it.)

. . . .

Here's the scoop according to Brandon Kelly, "You can't retrofit a successful Kickstarter campaign; either your audience exists on that platform or they don't."

Her campaign only hit 25 percent of its goal. But, missing it wasn't for lack of trying. She "researched crowdfunding extensively prior to our launch. Hearing again and again the necessity of having a base of followers prior to launch, we worked to build a Twitter following of nearly 5K in less than 5 months by daily content postings and purchased FB ads to increase our Page Likes to nearly 1K (all prior to launch).

"We hired a director to film our video," continues Brandon, "wrote the script ourselves and even developed a product video from the extra reels."

When it was all said and done, Brandon admitted—"Our idea did not resonate with the crowdfunding community."

. . . .

Why did you choose Kickstarter for your crowdfunding campaign? There are a number of choices out there that aren't as strict. What made them more attractive?

My partner and I chose Kickstarter because at the time of our launch it was getting the most press. We felt that in some ways Kickstarter was identified as the key crowdfunding brand. We also believed that due to some high profile campaigns—LaVar Burton's **Reading Rainbow** *drive and the* **Veronica Mars** *campaigns that even more people would be attracted to their platform.*

The risk, of course, with Kickstarter is that if you don't raise your goal, you receive none of the donations.

This risk seemed to be worth taking.

. . . .

I get what's in it for the person doing the Kickstarter campaign. What's harder for me to understand is what's in it for the guy who's backing you? What makes someone back a Kickstarter campaign? Is it the incentives you offer them at different levels, or is it just a need to be a part of something?

The campaigns that I have personally backed have been run by people I know personally. There is a personal tie of some sort that compelled me to give. This assertion is backed up by the results of our campaign; where nearly all of our donations were from people inside our network.

On the one hand we felt incredibly fortunate that people who we knew would be driven to give, but at the same time we never captured a broader audience within the crowdfunding space. I think it's important to note that not every product or idea will translate to the crowdfunding community but that shouldn't be a deterrent. You simply have to understand the crowdfunding audience is a specific segment.

Your customers may or may not be on that platform.

. . . .

How important are the incentives you give out for the different levels of contributions? I mean how attractive do you need to make those offers to conduct a successful crowdfunding campaign?

There is definitely a perception that at a center donation level you need to be able to offer something substantial. A few hundred dollars can go a long way on the free market to get you something of value. So when that donation level reaches a certain threshold, you need to have something tied to it with a perceived value.

. . . .

Can you tell me a little bit about the incentives you offered to contribute?

We were incredibly creative in how we positioned our gifts. Our product is made in the USA and is made of bamboo and has a silicone insert for hot tools. It is a well-crafted product and is not cheap to manufacture. That said, we really couldn't offer the product below a certain margin or else it would have defeated the purpose of the campaign. Beyond filming the video, assigning the gift structure was perhaps the most arduous aspect of the campaign.

. . . .

What was most effective? What do you wish you would have done different?

The most popular gift amount was between $50.00 and $100.00. The gifts offered at that price point were fairly low tech, a Tweet about your donation to our followers and a beauty product.

I think what drove this range in terms of popularity was they were amounts people felt comfortable donating. A lot of people throw $100 out there because they think it's an amount that might actually help out, but at the same time it won't leave a major dent in their purse strings.

....

What's more effective as an incentive, especially at the higher level, a high dollar value item, or personalized coaching or a group meeting with your backers?

I would say that for someone to donate a triple digit amount they need to have a real belief in what you're doing, and are also perhaps intrigued in some way by some aspect of the process. I believe the large donors want access to you in some way, whether it's to learn about your process or simply cache.

....

Everything I've read about running a Kickstarter campaign says you need to approach it like a real job. And, by that I mean you need to have a plan for what you want to accomplish, and you need to be working at it constantly? You have to pump people up, keep them aware of your goals, and update them on how you're doing. Can you talk about this a little?

Our campaign began months before it launched. We read some books on crowdfunding, studied it and then began the process of building a base of followers on FB and Twitter. By the time we launched our campaign we had nearly 5K Twitter followers and 1K FB followers; none of which we purchased, but all of which we gathered through developing interesting content and pushing our social media agenda daily.

Your launch shouldn't be the first time you are contacting or connecting with your audience about your project. We had been sharing pieces of detail all along the way, sharing pictures of our prototype, showing pictures of the factory where the product is produced, talking about any obstacles that we were facing that day. We hired a publicist to create a framework around our product, meaning, when we launched we wanted there to be content from other sources about our product and ourselves. She did a great job in connecting us with blogs, magazines and even television opportunities.

This work was all done months before we launched our campaign. That framework is still in place, so when we are ready to launch another product half of the work is already done for us.

. . . .

How long did you run your Kickstarter campaign for? If you had it to do over, would you run if for more or less time?

Our campaign was live for 45 days. I don't believe campaign duration affects the outcome.

. . . .

It's essential to hit your goal with Kickstarter, because if you don't—you don't get any money. With that in mind, should you ask for less than you need, or do you ask for what you need and come out punching?

We knew that we needed every penny of what we were asking for in order to proceed with phase 2 of our plan (the plastic mold). In order for us to have achieved and delivered on our promises we needed to hit that mark.

Asking for less would have really done us no good.

. . . .

Going back to the last question, it's great to hit your goal, but the real money seems to be in exceeding your goal. I see a lot of campaigns that double or even triple their original goals. I've also noticed those campaigns are constantly hitting it—on social media, on Kickstarter, and on their blogs and websites, plus adding additional incentives if they hit this push goal or that threshold. How important is this to being really successful?

Since we did not hit our goal I can't really speak to this point. In fact as it became apparent that our audience just wasn't there, we dialed back our media push and refocused our energies on the day to day promoting of our product and expanding its reach.

. . . .

Kickstarter encourages everyone to upload a video. How important is that to your success? And, how creative does that need to be?

I researched Kickstarter videos and it seemed the ones that made the most traction had videos. I spent about a month writing the script, and then another few weeks with the director paring it down.

For me the video was a way to show our audience who we are and also feature our product.

We hired a director to film our piece, and that was something I would do all over again.

Is it necessary to have a video? I can't really say because there are definitely times when I have scanned a page and seen enough detail and images to comprehend the campaign's goal. I think it's a personal decision, and is perhaps based on the tools at your disposal.

. . . .

What do you think attracts backers to a Kickstarter campaign? Is it your project? Is it how you present it and how imaginative you are? I guess what I'm really asking is—is there some kind of magic sauce you can sprinkle on your Kickstarter campaign that will virtually guarantee success, or is it more of a crapshoot?

If there is, we didn't find it! I think at core, with anything, you have to be authentic. If you believe in what you're doing, find a way to communicate your passion through the platform. Without that I don't think there can be traction.

. . . .

If you could only give someone getting ready to start their Kickstarter journey one piece of advice, what would it be?

Your Kickstarter campaign won't make or break your project. If you rely exclusively on this channel, you will more than likely be let down. Include crowdfunding as one in a series of efforts that you will leverage to achieve your goal.

Bonus Excerpt

*(Here's an excerpt from one of my newest books, **eBay Bookkeeping Made Easy**. This section focuses on how to use GoDaddy Bookkeeping to track your sales, expenses, and profits.)*

Getting started with GoDaddy Bookkeeping

GoDaddy Bookkeeping is available as an app you can download from eBay's applications bar. Amazon and Etsy sellers can check out the online version by visiting this link *http://www.godaddy.com/accounting/accounting-software.aspx?isc=gooob012&ci=87249.*

The service was originally known as Outright, and was taken over by GoDaddy last year. It's an online accounting solution that will serve the needs of most users. It automatically imports transaction data from your PayPal account, and posts it to the proper categories. Users can also synch their business credit cards and checking accounts with the service.

For sellers conducting business on multiple platforms GoDaddy Bookkeeping can import transaction data from eBay, Amazon and Etsy. It also works with several invoicing services including FreshBooks, Shoeboxed, and Harvest.

Here's the least you need to know. GoDaddy Bookkeeping is available in the *Applications* tab on your *My eBay* page. Hover your mouse over *Applications* until it shows Manage

Applications, click on this and scroll through the list of applications until you come to *Outright*. Click on *Outright*, and select *Try it Free*.

GoDaddy Bookkeeping is available as a monthly ($9.99) or yearly ($99.00) subscription. Choose your poison and follow the prompts to get started.

Overview

The first page you see is your account overview. It contains all of the basic information about your account. In the upper right corner it shows your yearly profit or loss so you can tell at a glance where you stand. Below this is a graph that charts your income and expenses, a pie chart that shows your current month's expenses, and then a list of open invoices.

Below this is a section that shows Invoice Activity. Most online sellers aren't going to use this feature as all of your invoicing is done through eBay, Amazon, Etsy, and your ecommerce storefronts. If you're running a side business where your customers pay through PayPal this is where you would bill your customers for products or services sold.

In the left hand column you'll see four small blue boxes. The first box is labeled *New This Week* and tracks your new sales, and any uncategorized expenses. To view your new transactions or uncategorized expenses click on the number, and it will take you to your general ledger.

The *Money I Have Box* lets you view the balances in your accounts – PayPal, Amazon, and any bank accounts you have connected.

The Money I Owe box shows your liabilities or the money you owe. Some of the accounts shown here are your eBay balance, and money owed to Amazon and Etsy for seller fees.

The last box is labeled *Taxes*. It shows you several key tax indicators for your business. The first line shows your estimated quarterly tax payment, and when it is due. The mileage line shows your year to date mileage expenses. When you click on mileage it takes you to your general ledger and lets you log your mileage. The last line shows your *Sales Tax Liability*, so you always know how much you owe.

Below the four blue boxes you should see two blue bars. *Add Account* lets you add your various seller accounts, PayPal Account, and any bank accounts you want to tie into GoDaddy Bookkeeping. *Refresh All* imports data from your connected accounts so that you're viewing the most recent information available.

If you scroll back up to the top of the page you'll see your six control tabs – Overview, Income, Expenses, Reports, Taxes, and Manage. When you click on any of these they open more program options.

Before I describe the control tabs there's one other item I should cover. Sometimes a tan bar will appear just below the control tab. It shows program alerts or problems GoDaddy Bookkeeping may be experiencing with your account. When you click on the Fix It highlight it will walk you through solving the problem so you can get your program up and running correctly again.

. . . .

You can view your profit & loss statement anytime by clicking on the *view details* tab underneath where it says *(Year) Profit & Loss* on the GoDaddy Bookkeeping *Overview* page.

Your Profit & Loss statement gives you a quick overview of the financial health of your business. The top section shows your sources of income, and the bottom section details your expenses. The final line shows your "bottom line," or the actual profit or loss your business is making.

The default view for your P & L is the previous twelve months, but you have the option to change that any time you'd like. Scroll up to the top of the page under *Profit & Loss* where you see *ending*. You can choose the ending month or year, or you can change the time period to day, week, month, quarter, or year. To return to the chart select the chart icon on the right hand side.

If you want to take a closer look at a transaction all of the items on your P & L are clickable. Select the one you want to examine and it will take you to the general ledger page for that category.

Moving back down to the bottom of the page you will see two tabs at the far right side. Export lets you transfer P & L information to a Microsoft Excel file. Selecting print will give you a hard copy of your P & L.

Income

The income tab lets you manage your online income accounts. When you click on income it takes you to your general ledger page for income, and you can view your most recent transactions.

Once again, all of the transactions displayed are clickable. If you want to edit a transaction select it, and make the needed corrections.

What I recommend here is to set up categories for all of your income transactions so you can track where your money is coming from. When GoDaddy Bookkeeping imports income transactions it brings all of them in under the general "sales" heading. If you're just selling on one venue, such as eBay or Amazon, that's not a problem. If you sell across multiple platforms it's important to know the source your money is coming from. This way you can take corrective action if a sales venue is underperforming.

The first thing you need to know is every time you make a sale GoDaddy Bookkeeping records it as two separate transactions. The merchandise portion is recorded under the "sales" heading. If postage was charged on the transaction it is recorded under the heading "shipping income."

If you want to add additional sales categories select a transaction, and then scroll down the page until you see a heading labeled *Good to Know*. Over to the right hand side you will see a link labeled *Manage Categories*. Select it. This shows you a chart of your current income categories. To add a category select *New income Category*. Categorize it as *Business* or *Nonbusiness*, and then name the new category. After doing this you need to select a tax category. To tie the category you created to sales you would choose *gross receipts or sales*. Select *create*, and your new category is ready to use.

To give you an idea about how to use this, I added the following categories to my income account – eBay sales, Amazon, Bonanaza, *eBid*, bidStart, Kindle, Create Space, and Audible. By doing this I can keep separate tabs on each of my sales channels. It gives me better control over my business, and allows me to spot patterns early as they're beginning to emerge.

After you set up your income categories you need to assign each individual transaction to the proper category. The easiest way to do this is from the Overview page. Select *view details* to see your P & L. Click on *sales* in the income section of your P & L. This will pull up all of your unassigned items. Select each item separately, and assign it to the proper income account. This step is pretty straightforward and should take just a few moments a day.

Whenever you're working on your P & L you also want to take a look at your uncategorized expenses. They're listed at the bottom of the P & L, just before you see your bottom line. Most items are categorized when they're imported, but there are usually a few uncategorized items, either because you purchased from a new supplier and GoDaddy Bookkeeping doesn't know how to classify it, or because the items you purchased from that supplier may fit into several different expense categories. Click on the individual unclassified transactions and assign them to the proper category.

If you do this every time you open your program it will only take a few minutes of your time, and it will ensure your P & L is up-to-date and accurate.

Expenses

When you select expenses it brings up the general ledger view for your business expenses.

Similar to the income category you can set up personalized categories to customize GoDaddy Bookkeeping for your business needs. Select an individual expense to enter the edit mode. Scroll down the page until you see the heading *Good to Know*. Move your mouse to the far right of the page and click on *manage categories*. Select *new expense category* and follow the prompts. Categorize the expense as a business or nonbusiness expense and name it. Scroll through the *tax category list* to tie your new expense to the proper category, and then select *Create*.

I would suggest setting up custom categories for your internet and cell phone providers, storage space rental, etc.

I find it useful to lump a few expense categories together. The main category I do this with is postage. I throw all of my shipping expenses in there – boxes, packing tape, stay free mailers, peanuts, you name it. The reason I do this is it makes it easier to compare my shipping expenses and shipping income. As long as the shipping income is equal to or more than my shipping expense, I know I'm on the right track. When they get out of whack it's time for an intervention to determine what went wrong.

With my other expenses my main concern is that they're consistent from month-to-month. If one month is way up without a similar bump in sales it's time to investigate what happened. Sometime it's a special purchase I had the opportunity to make; sometimes a number was entered wrong. The key thing is to watch your numbers and react quickly when you see that something is out of whack.

Reports

When you select reports it brings you to your Profit and loss statement. GoDaddy bookkeeping always shows you the chart first. Select *view as table* to see your P & L Statement.

If you're running a business you should know these numbers forwards and backwards. Growth is good, but I like to see consistent numbers across the board.

When I'm comparing my book sales numbers, the first thing I do is compare them with the last few months. If sales seem unusually low I take a peek at last year's numbers to see if it's a seasonal trend. You should do the same thing.

Online sales are always slower in summer. They normally pick up by late August and run strong through spring. February is a little iffy – it can go either way. The first half of November can be the same way waiting for Christmas buying to kick in.

Key point: Use your P & L to help forecast fluctuations in your business. Study it for trends, where sales are increasing or decreasing, or where expenses are rising. Put on your detective hat and figure out what's happening. Doing this will make you a better business person, and help your business to grow stronger over the long haul.

Taxes

The taxes section helps you with three specific areas.

1) It provides your Schedule C information to make tax time a breeze. Just transfer over the numbers and you're ready to file. Keep in mind you're still going to need a tax advisor or a good tax program like TurboTax Business or HR Block Business. GoDaddy Bookkeeping doesn't figure the home office deduction, tax credits, etc. They just provide you with the raw numbers to fill out your Schedule C.

2) GoDaddy tracks your sales taxes due, so it's easy to file and submit your state reports. As long as you have eBay, Amazon, and Etsy set up to collect sales tax in your state, GoDaddy Bookkeeping will track all of the information for you.

3) Every time you log into your account you are able to see your estimated tax payments and the date they are due. This way the due date and the amount you owe won't sneak up on you.

Manage

When you select manage it displays a list of all the accounts you have connected to GoDaddy Bookkeeping. If any of the accounts have errors you will see a tan bar displayed by them. Click on the blue *Fix It* link to take care of account issues.

If you want to connect more accounts, select *Add an Account* at the top of the page

. . . .

Good to know

You can easily reassign categories if something appears is mis-categorized.

Most often when this happens it's because the program does not recognize how to classify the transaction. To fix the problem select the item that needs to be classified. At the far right it will say uncategorized item, select the correct category from the drop down box, and press save.

You will also need to re-categorize items when you make a non-business related purchase. GoDaddy Bookkeeping has a *personal expense* category you can assign the item to so it is removed from your business records. If you sell a personal item and receive payment for an item through your PayPal account you can reassign it to the *personal income* category.

Best advice

Keep a close eye on your accounting program. Update it every few days. It's easier to catch errors when just a few items are displayed. If you let it go too long, a large list of items to re-categorize can seem overwhelming.

About the Author

My books offer short easy to read solutions to your ecommerce problems.

em can be read in under an hour. The information can be used to help you sell more products on eBay and Amazon, services on Fiverr, or eBooks on Amazon and Kindle.

Selling on line isn't a mystery. It doesn't even have to be difficult.

It's really all about getting started. Many people I've talked with have this crazy fear about putting things up for sale on eBay and Amazon. They think they have to do this and do that; they worry they don't know enough about what they're doing to do it right; they wonder what they should sell; and they worry about whether they can even do it or not.

That's where my books come in.

They take you hand-in-hand and walk you through getting started selling on eBay, Amazon, and Fiverr. They show you how to market your Kindle book.

My goal is to help you over the speed bumps, so you can be more successful from the get-go.

What are you waiting for?

Most of my books are available as audio books, so if you prefer to listen rather than read, be sure to check them out.

August 18th, 2015

Nick Vulich
Davenport, Iowa

Books by Nick Vulich

Don't like history? You're probably reading the wrong books.

Read this book, and you're gonna think, wow! Why didn't somebody tell me that? American history is full of strange paradoxes, and that's what makes it so interesting.

The truth is much of what we learn about history is a series of little white lies that over time have grown into tall tales.

* Why doesn't everyone know the Boston Massacre wasn't really a massacre? Subsequent testimony proved the soldiers fired in self-defense. The King Street riot was started by a group of four street thugs who got their rocks off attacking lone British soldiers. Sam Adams and Paul Revere twisted it into a massacre.

* And, if you think the Boston Tea Party was a response to British taxes that raised the price of tea in the colonies, think again. The Tea Act of 1773 actually reduced

the price of tea paid by the colonists. The people hurt by the Tea Act were the smugglers. The lower price of tea undercut their business, and ensured that the East India Company would have a monopoly on tea.

* The South Carolina Nullification Congress of 1832 was a harbinger of things to come. The question was if a state disagrees with a federal law, does it have the right to nullify it, and disregard that law? Vice-president John C. Calhoun argued state's rights superseded federal laws. President Andrew Jackson believed to his dying day that Calhoun was a damned traitor, and that he should have strung him up from the nearest branch.

* The Black Hawk War was a mix-up of frontier madness, mayhem, and murder. Illinois Governor John Reynolds called out the militia and raised thousands of volunteer troops. General Winfield Scott marched his regulars half way across the country to Fort Armstrong at Rock Island. Lieutenant Colonel Zachary Taylor led a group of infantrymen in the fighting. In the end, it was a massacre that nearly wiped out the Sac tribe.

* In the fall of 1845 President Polk offered Mexico five million dollars if they would recognize the Southwestern Boundary of Texas at the Rio Grande. When Mexico refused his offer Polk decided to force the issue. He sent General Zachary Taylor and 3,000 troops to Corpus Christi, Texas. In March of 1846 General Taylor moved his forces into the disputed territory between the Rio Grande and Nueces

Rivers. Soon after that, Mexico was provoked into a war with the United States.

* It has been said that James Buchanan was a "weak, timid, old man" who didn't do anything to prevent the Southern states from seceding. Some historians have even gone so far as to declare Buchanan was an "accessory after the fact." He was a president, Southern sympathizer, and traitor. But, was he?

* Imagine what it would be like to wake up, flip on the morning news, and discover Bradley Cooper or Ashton Kutcher assassinated President Obama. That's what happened in 1865. People were shocked when they learned John Wilkes Booth killed President Lincoln. Booth was one of the most popular actors of his day. He was young, just twenty-six years old, considered one of the most attractive men in America. At the time he killed Lincoln, Booth was pulling down $20,000 a year as an actor (that's roughly $300,000 in 2015 money). And, yet—he sacrificed it all for his political beliefs. What was going on in the mind of John Wilkes Booth?

I could tell you more, but you get the idea. Things aren't always what they appear to be. There are two sides to every story. All that stuff your teacher told you in school—it may, or may not be true.

Read this book, and decide for yourself which version you should believe.

Nick Vulich

MAKE MORE MONEY

5 Moves You Need to Make Today to Sell More Stuff on eBay

Do you want to make more money selling on eBay?

1. Do you ever find yourself looking at successful sellers on eBay and thinking – They know something I don't.
2. They've probably got some kind of inside connection that lets them get products cheaper than I ever could.
3. They've already got the market sewed up, there's not any business left for me.

Have you ever told yourself –

1. If I had a little more money, I could buy the inventory I need to make a killing on eBay.
2. If I had a little more time, I'd be able to list enough items to be successful.
3. If I had a little more information, I could pick a killer product that would make me a million dollars selling on eBay.

Sounds crazy, doesn't it?

Every eBay book out there tells you the same thing. You need to find a great product that you can purchase at a reasonable price, and sell for a huge profit. If they don't tell you that, they tell you how easy it is to source product at garage sales, yard sales, flea markets, or the local thrift stores. And, my absolute favorite is the books that list 1001 things you can sell on eBay to make a huge profit. The only problem is half of the items they list are things you're unlikely to find – anywhere. Or, if you do a little research, you discover that fabulous selling price they told you was a one-time thing. The item is actually selling for much less now, if it is even selling at all.

Some books talk about drop shipping, or buying inventory wholesale from secret suppliers they use to make a killing selling on eBay and Amazon. Another eBay expert marketing his advice on Craigslist shows you how to source products on Amazon to sell on eBay. The secret is to discover fast selling items on Amazon, and list them for sale on eBay. When you make a sale on eBay – buy it on Amazon, and have the seller ship it to your customer. Of course, you need to purchase their entire system to make it work - $19.95 per month.

I've investigated all of these scams. And, yes – they are scams. If you buy from the majority of the "Special" wholesalers and drop shippers, you're going to discover most of the items they offer are selling on eBay for less than you paid "wholesale."

No matter what anyone tells you, selling on eBay isn't easy. It's not a sure thing. For every item that sells, another one or two items go unsold, or sell for far less than you hoped for.

eBay 2015 tells it like it is

I'm not going to tell you what to sell, where to buy it, or which items to buy. When someone guarantees you a profit they're normally feeding you a line of bull-hockey.

There's no hype, no BS, and no false promises. **eBay 2015** discusses the new eBay Seller Standards and how they affect you. It covers the problems eBay sellers encounter choosing which products to sell, how to keep accurate records, and how to ship items inexpensively and efficiently.

Learn how to –

1. Plan for success
2. Choose a niche
3. Ship like a pro
4. Sell international
5. Track your income and expenses

Nick Vulich

SELL SHIP REPEAT

**Why Your Stuff Isn't Selling
And What You Can Do About It**

Selling on eBay isn't a game

You need to have a plan

eBay 2014 walks you through what it takes to sell on eBay. It answers all of your questions, and gives you ideas about how to get started and grow your eBay business.

Do you ever wonder how some sellers can grow a strong thriving business, while others barely scrape by?

Many times, I've watched two sellers as they are first starting out on eBay. Both sellers offer the exact same products and prices, yet one business skyrockets to the top of the charts selling thousands of items per month. The other business struggles to sell ten or fifteen items per month. They might even have the same basic look to their listings. On the face of it, it doesn't make sense.

Why does one eBay seller prosper, while another falls behind?

Is it a matter of luck? Does one eBay seller catch all of the breaks, while another is stuck holding doo doo? Believe it or not, many struggling sellers believe this. They think it's all a matter of luck. But, you and I know better. Don't we?

Sellers who succeed on eBay play by different rules

They don't leave anything to chance. They know that success requires a plan. You don't just move from Point A to Point B. You need to make it happen. And, that's what this book is all about. It gives you a strategy for selling on eBay.

You will learn

1. How to write titles that draw buyers into your listings and help them find what you are selling
2. How to take picture that show buyers what they need to know to say "This is the item I'm looking for!"
3. The anatomy of a great listing. What you should say. How you should say it. What not to say.
4. Why you need to stop guessing at prices for your items, and how to determine realistic prices that customers are willing to pay.
5. The smart way to ship your items so you can get your packages to your customers safely and on time.
6. How to rock customer service, and motivate your customers to leave five star feed-back every time.
7. how to deal with eBay's constant string of updates and changes

Still not convinced?

Consider this.

- There are over 149 million active buyers on eBay.
- Last year they spent over $83 billion dollars on everything from paperclips to new cars and custom helicopters.

- Hundreds of thousands of small sellers are making $500, a $1000, even $2500 every month working part time from their kitchen table or garage.

How about you?

Are you making your fair share?

If not, this book will help you understand - selling on eBay isn't a game. You need to have a plan.

- **Get serious about your eBay selling**
- **Order this book - TODAY!**
- **Make more sales tomorrow - and everyday**